PiCa
PaU$_2$

Animal Friends of Pica Pau 2
Gather All 20 Original Amigurumi Characters

© 2020 Yan Schenkel and Meteoor BV (BE0550756201)

Fifth print run: April 2022

First published June 2020 by
Meteoor Books, Antwerp, Belgium
www.meteoorbooks.com
hello@meteoorbooks.com

Have you made characters with patterns from this
book? Share your creations on
www.amigurumi.com/3100 or on
Instagram with #animalfriendsofpicapau2.

Photography: Yan Schenkel & Matías Gorostegui
Illustrations: Yan Schenkel

Printed and bound by Grafistar

ISBN 9789491643354
D/2020/13.531/2

*A catalogue record for this book is available from the
Royal Library of Belgium.*

YAN SCHENKEL

ANIMAL FRIENDS OF

METEOOR BOOKS

INDEX

INTRODUCTION

Even now, I cannot believe that I have written my third book. It's surreal. And writing the preliminary words to this book is still one of the hardest parts. There are so many thoughts I'd like to pour on the page, feelings of gratitude and excitement, an almost tearful 'thank you' to the people supporting me (yes, I'm talking about you!) as well as a big sigh of relief now that my job is done (but is it ever?). It's been a rollercoaster ride again.

Keeping my introduction clean and simple would be a lot easier, but I'm not working in sales, and the emotional value of the book in front of you is so big to me that, if I'm not careful, the words just keep flowing out of my pen. I've tried to curb the word flow, and I hope you'll flow along for a bit.

In my previous book, I wrote about my life with crochet (if you do not have it, you should go out and buy it now! Maybe I should work in sales after all). For me, writing a pattern book starts with an almost irresistible urge, a need to make and share my makes with you. I started writing this third book when I was 4 months pregnant with my third child. I don't want to hide the stress, the headaches, the lack of sleep that accompanied me in those months … These things are tied up with the delights of being a mother again, but they have also weighed down my crochet hook and writing pen at times. Nevertheless, I've learned that getting stuck on a bit and feeling frustrated can give you a really big push, you can feel the energy welling up inside you as you think to yourself 'I AM going to tackle this'. And that's how we learn to move forward, both in crochet and in life.

I remember a book chapter by Tina Fey (who's a North American comedian, writer, producer, and a thousand other things) where she was talking about her stress levels while working on one of her iconic comedy TV shows. In her book, she wrote page after page about her never-ending work hours, her anxiety and the need to put other people's expectations first … And then she drew a diagram comparing her stress levels to those of the hard-working people in the mines or in fast-food restaurants on a busy Friday night. That's when it hit her that it was ok to complain, but that there are a bunch of jobs that are way more stressful. I often feel the same.

Everyone is trying their very best, especially when it comes to juggling work with the huge demands of kids who are busy testing the limits of their world (and yours). So here's a big shout-out to all the people working hard, away from the spotlights: you're doing a great job, and we know you make amazing efforts, even if you don't always show or share them.

My job can look so romantic from a distance, and I must confess I'm struggling with that idea, because it's very much a job, with both good days and not-so-good days. On social media, you see the idyllic image of hands (perfectly manicured) holding a hook with grace, while a perfect cup of coffee frames the picture. You see the most gorgeous yarns, the well-behaved pets and an almost sublime light giving the scene a perfect filter. You do not see the backache after a long day of photographing, or the tiredness from trying to keep your kid entertained while tackling your to-do list. These things are not in the picture, and yet they are, they're right there as well!

I'm grateful that this job has been so good to me. It has allowed me to express myself creatively, to meet wonderful people around the world, and to support my family, all by designing and crocheting these quirky creatures of mine. I'm from Argentina, so I express my emotions freely (why, complaining could even be our national sport), but I'm grateful that sometimes

absurd amounts of yarn and crocheted animals take over my house. I'm truly happy with all of your messages of love and support. I'm so proud when you show off your creations and share your achievements and joy, it's beyond words (though you wouldn't say that it's 'beyond words', reading this wordy introduction of mine). I'm grateful for being part of this enormous group of crafters who support each other. I'm grateful for all of you who ask me advice or just check in to see how I'm doing, who offer me kind words or even their help to test a new pattern or translate another. And I'm grateful for my huge extended family, who – along with the family under my own roof – encourage me on a daily basis to continue this incredible job of making characters for you to enjoy. So please, take your time and enjoy this book to your heart's content, I couldn't be happier now that it has reached your hands!

And because my inner nerd never tires: I hope this book is a worthy successor, my 'Empire Strikes Back' (instead of my 'Attack of the Clones'). Enjoy!

When crocheting my patterns

As with my previous books, I planned this book as a learning journey, adding a little challenge to each character so that you may feel comfortable crocheting anything you want once you reach the end of the book.

I'll show you my way of making toys, my tricks … and some questionable acquired habits: I hold the hook like a knife (which looks pretty ugly in the pictures), I make some stitches in an unconventional way (the illustrious X-shaped single crochet), I prefer to sew on the snout before stuffing the toy's body and I do not like the "invisible" decrease. But that's me. You can always find another way to achieve the same – or better – results.

If you know everything there is to know about crocheting amigurumi, or if you are feeling brave, you can start with any character you want. But if you are just starting or you haven't reached that level of confidence yet, I strongly recommend you to crochet the toys in the suggested order. With each pattern you'll be learning something new, something extra that will allow you to start the next one armed with all the tools needed to acquire a new technique without feeling (so) frustrated. That's my way of helping you on a pleasant crochet journey. Always remember that being patient and paying attention to what you are doing are just as important (or even more so) as the tools and materials you're using.

I should also give you a heads-up: the finished toys are pretty big. I use a fairly thick yarn and I like to make creatures that are big enough so you do not have to peer at the details. I used less than 100 grams of every main color and rather small amounts of the secondary colors. Do not feel tied to my choices of yarn though. I used worsted weight cotton yarn for most of the characters, but any weight of cotton, acrylic or wool can be used as a substitute (just do not forget to use the right crochet hook accordingly).

Every pattern can be a starting point for another one. So play with them, modify them as you please and adapt them to meet your needs. And most important of all, have fun. There are already too many stressful things in life and although you may encounter a few bumps in the road (we all have our fair amount of crochet failures), do not forget to have a good time and enjoy the alchemy of yarns and hooks producing huggable creatures.

Amigurumi gallery

With each pattern, I have included a URL and a QR code that will take you to that character's dedicated online gallery. Share your finished amigurumi, find inspiration in the color and yarn choices of your fellow crocheters and enjoy the fun of crocheting. Simply follow the link or scan the QR code with your mobile phone. Phones with iOS will scan the QR code automatically in camera mode. For phones with Android you may need to install a QR Reader app first.

TOOLS AND SUPPLIES

Every experienced crocheter has her/his favorite tools and materials, in addition to a well-formed opinion on the best techniques and the things you should always avoid. Of course, as in any other aspect of life, we do not always agree. Although each one of us has their own taste and point of view, we all acknowledge that one of the most wonderful things about crochet is that with basic tools and a strand of yarn you can create almost anything. The only thing that you need to keep in mind is that high-quality hooks and yarn can save you hours of frustration. Whenever possible, choose quality over quantity. Hooks and needles do have the habit of getting lost, so make sure you always have a backup, especially of the ones you love and use all the time.

CROCHET HOOK

Note: I didn't try all the hooks available on the market and it's impossible for me to estimate exactly what kind of hook will be the best for you. This is a quest you must follow all by yourself. But I do not want to leave you entirely in the dark, so I'm going to tell you what I have learned these past 11 years crocheting toys.

You may have noticed that, apart from different sizes, crochet hooks come in different materials. The choice for a material depends on your own preference. However, if you are planning to use cotton yarn, I strongly recommend working with **stainless steel** or **aluminum** hooks. Aluminum hooks are a great choice as they slip easily between stitches, are super light and come in the widest range of sizes. The thinnest aluminum hooks (less than 4 mm) might bend if you apply a lot of pressure, which happens when crocheting tightly. To avoid this, choose the ones with silicon, plastic, wood or bamboo handles or go for a stainless-steel hook (my personal favorite, as I tend to be a little rough on them).

Wooden and **bamboo** hooks are gorgeous and some brands have the most incredibly smooth finish, but I only recommend them if you are going to work with thicker yarns or crochet garments with looser stitches. The same goes for **plastic** and **acrylic** hooks, they're sometimes used to work with thicker materials, such as T-shirt yarn. I haven't tried these, as they seem less sturdy.

Besides the material of the hook, it's always wise to check the anatomy of the hook. As for the **point**: I prefer a rounded and blunt tip, with no rough edges so it doesn't split the yarn and slides through the stitches easily.

Also pay attention to the **throat** of the crochet hook. This part does the actual hooking (catching) of the yarn and allows you to pull it through the stitches and loops. You need a hook with a throat large enough to grab the yarn that you're work-ing with, but small enough to prevent the previous loop from sliding off. This is especially important when crocheting toys, as you are going to use a crochet hook two or three sizes smaller than recommended for your yarn.

Another thing to keep in mind is the **handle**. I can say almost without a doubt that this is the most personal decision of all. In my case, as I hold the crochet hook like a knife (see page 18), I prefer to use crochet hooks without big handles. But if you hold it like a pencil, you will probably prefer the ones with an ergonomic or a rubber handle.

Hooks are like pens: we can crochet with any hook until we find the one that changes our lives. Yes, it's a bit dramatic, but it's true. And if it doesn't change your life, it will definitely change the way you crochet, especially if you do it all day long.

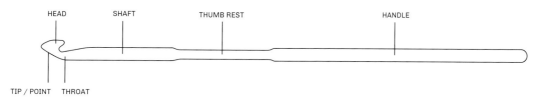

TIP / POINT   THROAT   HEAD   SHAFT   THUMB REST   HANDLE

Sizes

As a basic guide, a thicker thread needs a bigger hook and makes a larger stitch. If you crochet loosely, use a smaller hook to tighten your crochet fabric, and if you crochet tightly, use a larger hook to loosen your fabric. The hook size should be what's comfortable for you to use to obtain the desired result. It's easier to change the size of the hook than to modify the pressure you apply, as everyone tends to have a "natural" tension.

Hook sizes are indicated using different, land-specific systems, drawing on either numbers or letters or a combination of both. In the table below you can find the three most common systems in use: the metric system, the UK system and the US system. In this book I mention the metric and US size of the hook.

Crochet hook conversions

METRIC	UK	US
2 mm	14	-
2.25 mm	13	B-1
2.5 mm	12	-
2.75 mm	-	C-2
3 mm	11	-
3.25 mm	10	D-3
3.5 mm	9	E-4
3.75 mm	-	F-5
4 mm	8	G-6
4.5 mm	7	7
5 mm	6	H-8
5.5 mm	5	I-9
6 mm	4	J-10
6.5 mm	3	K-10.5
7 mm	2	-
8 mm	0	L-11
9 mm	00	M-13
10 mm	000	N-15

YARN

We can use almost any material that can be worked into a thread: wool, cotton, string, ribbon, fabric, leather, wire, even plastic bags or paper. Each kind of thread has its pros and cons. Allow yourself to experiment with different materials, it's the best way to learn and find what you like the most and what is most suitable for your project.

Always try to buy quality yarns, ones that are pleasant to the touch and comfortable to crochet with.

Cotton

Cotton is the most commonly used fiber for crocheting toys and, in my opinion, the one that gives the best result. It's a natural vegetable fiber made from cellulose. (Other threads composed of vegetable fibers are flax, jute, rayon, bamboo, hemp, etc.)

In addition to being a hypoallergenic material, cotton is extremely durable, easy to wash, very soft, and has plenty of color options to choose from! This thread has practically no elasticity, which is something you definitely want when making toys (so the toy keeps its shape). However, because of this lack of elasticity, the hook may not slide easily and sometimes, as cotton yarn is made up of several strands, the thread can be frayed by the hook.

You can find cotton threads in a variety of presentations: from more "rustic" and opaque ones, over shiny, mercerized cottons and combed ones (with threads that were combed to remove short fibers, to obtain more strength and softness).

Wools

Another type of natural fibers are the protein ones, the fibers that come from animal hair, like sheep's wool, alpaca, angora and mohair, or from insect secretions, like silk.

These yarns are more elastic than yarns made of vegetable fibers, so you have to keep in mind that toys made with this kind of yarn might lose their shape over time.

Beginners should avoid the hairiest ones (like angora and mohair), because the furry texture hides the

structure of the fabric, making it harder to know where to insert the hook.

Synthetic fibers

Made of polymers, synthetic yarns are usually spun into a thread that resembles the texture and feel of animal fibers. Although they're cheaper and slip on the hook nicely, some tend to pill (form little fuzzballs on the surface) and create static. Nevertheless, it's one of the most commonly chosen yarns to make toys with because of the incredible range of colors. I myself am not such a big fan of the glossy finish, but, like everything in life, it's a matter of taste.

Fiber weight

The yarn's weight is its thickness, in other words the relationship between the weight and the number of meters. For example, a super fine thread used for lace may have about 800 meters in 100 grams, while a jumbo yarn, like the ones used for those super chunky blankets, may have less than 100 meters in the same weight. Internationally, most books and yarn manufacturers rely on standard terms to indicate yarn weight. The number of strands (or PLY) is mentioned optionally because an increase of plies doesn't mean that the yarn will be heavier (in fact, an 8-ply yarn formed of tightly twisted plies may be thinner than a loosely twisted 6-ply yarn).

NUMBER	NAME	TYPES OF YARN IN CATEGORY	PLY	m/100 gr	RECOMMENDED HOOK SIZE FOR GARMENTS (mm)
0	Lace	Fingering	1-2 ply	600-800 or more	1.5 - 2.5
1	Super Fine	Sock, Fingering, Baby	3-4 ply	350-600	2.25 - 3.5
2	Fine	Sport, Baby	5 ply	250-350	3.5 - 4.5
3	Light	DK (double knitting), Light Worsted	8 ply	200-250	4.5 - 5.5
4	Medium	Worsted, Afghan, Aran	10-12 ply	120-200	5.5 - 6.5
5	Bulky	Chunky, Craft, Rug	12-16 ply	100-130	6.5 - 9
6	Super Bulky	Super Bulky, Super Chunky, Roving		Less than 100	9 and larger
7	Jumbo	Jumbo, Roving		Less than 100	15 and larger

Note: *The yarn weight and the hook should always relate to each other. Most importantly, always keep in mind that when making toys, you'll have to use a hook two or three sizes smaller than what is recommended for crocheting a garment (as stated in the table above). After all, we want a dense fabric that won't allow the stuffing to show through.*

OTHER ESSENTIAL TOOLS AND SUPPLIES

Yarn and tapestry needles are used for joining motifs, sewing and finishing pieces. They have a blunt tip, so you don't split the thread or the crochet stitches. They also have a large eye that allows thicker yarns to pass through.

I have a thing for **scissors**, so I have a lot of them in different shapes and sizes. Choose a small, lightweight pair of scissors with sharp points.

A **stitch marker**, as the name suggests, is a tool used to mark a stitch. You can find them in a variety of shapes and qualities. Alternatively, you can use paper clips, safety pins or hair clips to help you indicate the round, row or any location on the worked piece.
When crocheting in rounds, always mark the first (or the last) stitch of the previous round.

I don't use a lot of **pins**, but they come in handy when you have to attach the head or limbs to the body of a toy. Try to get plastic or glass-headed ones: they're easy to spot in your crochetwork and their large head prevents them from slipping through the stitches.

For **stuffing** I always use polyester fiberfill, the same filling used to stuff cushions. It's easy to find in any craft shop, and it's inexpensive, washable and hypoallergenic. Stuffing a toy can be trickier than it seems: overstuffing might stretch the fabric and show through. Too little stuffing gives the toy a sad look, as if the poor thing was deflated. Try to insert small amounts at a time, adding more at a slow pace until you get the right look.

There is a great variety of extra elements to decorate crocheted toys: plastic eyes and noses in all colors and sizes, buttons, bows, ribbons, etc. For my characters, I only use **plastic safety eyes**. They have two parts: the front with a straight or threaded rod, plus a washer that goes inside the toy. If it's fastened correctly, it's practically impossible to remove. Be careful that the eye is where you want it to be before attaching it! If you're afraid that a tenacious child can pull them out, you can apply universal glue before placing them on the toy. Alternatively, you can embroider the facial features (especially if children are under the age of three).

TENSION FOR CLOTHES AND ACCESSORIES: THE GAUGE

The gauge is the number of stitches and rows obtained per inch/cm. It's also referred to as the tension. The size of your stitch will vary depending on the yarn weight, fiber, hook size and, of course, your personal tension. You may even have a different tension throughout the day, depending on your mood, or the same yarn weight could produce different gauges in different colors.

To make sure you will get the result you want, you have to use the exact same type of yarn fiber, yarn color and crochet hook size for your swatch and your project. If you can maintain your mood, that's a plus (please message me to explain how you manage to do so).

When crocheting toys, we don't need to know the gauge, we simply need to use the right hook to get a tight fabric.

When you are using different yarn weights for the same toy, making a swatch could spare you a fair amount of frustration (even more so if you are making clothes for your character). To make a swatch, you crochet a small piece, usually a 4x4 inches / 10x10 cm square. Since we don't need to be as accurate as when making clothes for people (or pets), you can make a smaller swatch and calculate the number of stitches and rows you need to get to 4 inches/ 10 cm.

The characters in this book have been made with Pica Pau Combed Cotton yarn (available from picapauyan.com). These are the gauges I obtained using the yarn and hook indicated in the patterns.

Pica Pau worsted weight 100% combed cotton yarn, 100g/170m per ball
- 20 stitches and 22 rows for 4 inches/10 cm "X shaped" single crochet in rows (flat fabric), with a C-2/2.75 mm hook
- 21 stitches and 22 rounds for 4 inches/10 cm "X shaped" single crochet in rounds (a tube), with a C-2/2.75 mm hook
- 18 stitches and 15 rows for 4 inches/10 cm half double crochet between stitches in rows, with a C-2/2.75 mm hook

Pica Pau fingering weight 100% combed cotton yarn, 50g/220m per ball
- Using 2 strands, 23 stitches and 24 rounds for 4 inches/ 10 cm "X shaped" single crochet in rounds (a tube), with a C-2/2.75 mm hook
- Using 1 strand, 25 stitches and 19 rows for 4 inches/10 cm half double crochet in rows (flat), with a C-2/2.75 mm hook
- Using 2 strands, 20 stitches and 15 rows for 4 inches/10 cm half double crochet in rows (flat), with a C-2/2.75 mm hook
- Using 2 strands, 19 stitches and 14 rows for 4 inches/10 cm half double crochet in rows (flat), with a D-3/3.25 mm hook

CROCHET INTRODUCTION

HOLD THE HOOK AND YARN (HAND POSITION)

Holding a new tool can be a little tricky, but a couple of hours of practice and a bit of patience will do the trick. If you already know how to crochet and you feel comfortable with it, stick to it! If you're learning, try as many ways as you like, so you can find the one most suitable for you. Usually, we handle the hook with the same hand we use to write, but it's not a rule. No matter how you hold the hook and the yarn, the most important thing you need to know is that there is no "best way" and definitely no "right way".

Pencil grip
Hold the hook as you would a pencil, grasping the hook between your thumb and index finger, in the middle of the flat section (the thumb rest).

Knife grip
Hold the hook in the same manner as you would hold a knife, grasping it between your thumb and index finger, resting the end of the hook against your palm.

Hold the yarn
The free hand is used to control the thread and hold the work. There are several methods to hold the yarn, and everyone has his or her preferred way. You only have to keep in mind that you have to maintain a steady tension while crocheting.
Holding the yarn is the real deal: you will need to practice controlling the thread and make the tension feel comfortable and natural. It's also important to keep this hand "in shape", because it's the one that's going to be stressed. Try to exercise before and after crocheting. I know it sounds almost impossible, but please, try not to crochet too many hours in a row!

STITCHES

There are only a handful of basic stitches and although the variations and combinations are endless, you only need to master a few to make the patterns in this book. I will explain the stitches that I've learned throughout the years and still use. Always remember that you can and should adapt the techniques to your own needs and possibilities.

SLIP KNOT

The slip knot is the first loop you'll need to make on your hook to start crocheting.

1   Make a loop shape with the tail end of the yarn. Insert the hook into it and draw another loop through.
2   Pull the yarn tail to tighten the loop around the hook.

The slip knot does not count as a stitch.

A little confession: when I took my first steps in crochet, I didn't know about the slip knot, so I made a regular knot on my hook ... I still do (but don't tell anyone).

CHAIN STITCH *(abbreviation: ch)*

This stitch is the basis for most crochetwork: if you are working in rows, your first row will be chain stitches, known as a foundation chain. The chain stitch is also used to join motifs and as a turning stitch.

1   Holding the slip knot, wrap the yarn from back to front around the hook. This movement is called "yarn over". You can wind the yarn over the hook or twist the hook to go under the yarn.
2   Draw the hook backward to pull the yarn through the loop on the hook (the slip knot).
3   You will form a new loop, this is your first chain stitch.
Repeat the previous steps to form as many chain stitches as required.

Note: *It's crucial to hold the yarn tail firmly to prevent it from spinning around the hook every time you try to yarn over.*

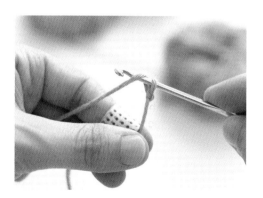

Foundation chain

This is the string of chain stitches you have to crochet if you want to make a flat fabric worked in rows. It's the equivalent of casting on when you start knitting.

Note: To help maintain an even foundation chain, keep changing your grip on the crocheted chains, so you are always holding them near the hook.

Turning chain

When crocheting in rows, these are the chain stitches you have to make to bring the hook up to the height of the stitches you are crocheting. Each stitch has a corresponding number of turning chains:
– a row of single crochet: 1 turning chain
– a row of half double crochet: 2 turning chains
– a row of double crochet: 3 turning chains

Note: When counting stitches, do not count the slip knot or the loop on the hook (this is the working loop). The easiest way to count stitches is to look at the plaited tops. Remember to count your stitches now and then to make sure you have the exact number of stitches required in the pattern.

INSERT THE HOOK (PLACEMENT OF STITCHES)

With the exception of chains, for all crochet stitches the hook needs to be inserted into existing stitches. The point of the hook must look down or sideways, so the hook doesn't snag the yarn or the fabric. When picking up stitches, you can insert the hook in three different places: the back loop, the front loop or under both loops.
– BOTH LOOPS: insert the hook under both loops of the stitch in the row or round below. This is the most common way to crochet and the preferred method when the pattern doesn't specify another way.
– FRONT LOOP ONLY *(abbreviation FLO)*: insert the hook under the one loop closest to you.
– BACK LOOP ONLY *(abbreviation BLO)*: insert the hook under the one loop furthest away from you. This leaves the front loop as a horizontal bar. It's used for aesthetic effects or to re-join the yarn.

SLIP STITCH (abbreviation: slst)

This stitch has no height and is hardly ever used on its own to make a crochet fabric. Instead, it's generally used to join ends into a circle, join pieces, finish a piece or move across the stitches to another part of the work.

1. Insert the hook through both loops of the next stitch (on the foundation chain: insert in second chain from the hook).
2. Yarn over the hook and draw through both loops at once. You have now completed one slip stitch.

Note: When working slip stitches in the last round or row to finish or embellish a piece, try to work the stitches a little more loosely to avoid puckering the fabric.

Join a chain ring with a slip stitch (tubular foundation chain)

1. Insert the hook into the first chain. Make sure the chain is not twisted.
2. Yarn over and draw the yarn through both loops on the hook at once.

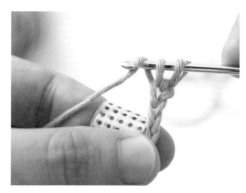

SINGLE CROCHET *(abbreviation: sc)*

The single crochet is THE stitch for working crocheted toys because it's the only one that results in a closed and tight fabric. The single crochet not only works excellently to maintain the shape of the toy, but also avoids that stuffing will show through (as long as we don't stuff it too much).

In rows (flat fabric)

Start from a foundation chain.
1 Insert the hook in the second chain stitch from the hook. Yarn over the hook.
2 Pull the yarn through the chain stitch. Now you have two loops on the hook. Yarn over the hook again.
3 Draw the hook backward to pull the yarn through both loops at once. One loop remains on the hook, and you have completed one single crochet stitch.
4 Insert the hook into the next stitch and continue crocheting into every chain stitch.
5 At the end of a row, make one turning chain and turn the work horizontally to begin the next row. Crochet one single crochet stitch into the next stitch (not counting the turning chain), inserting the hook through both loops of the stitch in the row below. Continue crocheting until the end of the row and repeat.

Note: *When crocheting in rows, it doesn't matter if you chain and turn or turn and chain, but be consistent with the way you turn your work.*

In a spiral (a tube)

Start from a foundation chain. Make sure your chain isn't twisted and put the hook through the first chain stitch. Close into a ring by making one slip stitch in the first chain.

1   Continue crocheting one single crochet into each chain stitch until you reach the beginning. Work a single crochet into the first single crochet you made (do not close the round with a slst). This is when the stitch marker comes in handy: place it into the single crochet you just made.

2   Continue working single crochet stitches until you reach the stitch marker. Remove the marker and work a single crochet in this stitch. Replace the marker into the stitch you just made and repeat.

Yarn over.

Yarn under.

Difference between V and X single crochet

If you're an experienced crocheter you might have noticed that my stitches look slightly different from what you're accustomed to. Instead of wrapping the yarn over my crochet hook, I wrap it under my crochet hook, that is, I "yarn under". By doing this, I get an X-shaped single crochet stitch instead of a V-shaped single crochet stitch.

Apart from the different look, there are a few more differences you should know about.

– **Size:** X-shaped single crochet is much tighter, so the result will be smaller. Vice versa, the fabric made using V-shaped single crochet is more fluid/elastic, so the toy will be softer. For example, if I make a circle of 60 stitches using X-shaped single crochet, my circle will be about 3.3 inches / 8.5 cm in diameter. If I make it using V-shaped single crochet, its diameter is about 4 inches / 10 cm.

– **How the stitches seem to turn around:** V-shaped single crochet stitches move a little in each round, so your crochetwork appears to turn to one side. X-shaped single crochet is less likely to do this, which will give nicer results when crocheting jacquard.

– **How the stripe patterns look:** X-shaped single crochet looks like a half double crochet when making stripes in different colors.

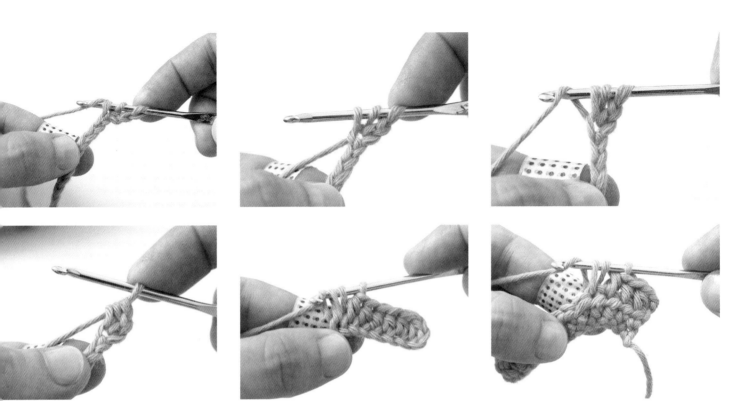

HALF DOUBLE CROCHET (abbreviation: hdc)

As its name indicates, this stitch is halfway between a single crochet and a double crochet in height. Being a looser stitch, the fabric made with half double crochet is more fluid and is excellent for working toy garments.

In rows (flat fabric)

Start from a foundation chain. The first two chain stitches of the foundation chain are the turning chain for the first row.

1 Yarn over. Insert the hook into the third chain from the hook and yarn over again.
2 Draw the yarn through one loop only. You now have three loops on the hook.
3 Yarn over again and draw through all three loops on the hook.
4 You have completed the first half double crochet stitch.
5 Continue crocheting into every chain stitch.
6 At the end of the row, make two turning chains and turn the work horizontally to begin the next row. Crochet one half double crochet in the third stitch from the hook, inserting the hook under both loops of the stitch in the row below. Repeat until you reach the end of the row.

Note: *I usually work between the stitches when working half double or double crochet in rounds. It creates an open effect that makes for a more elastic fabric. To do this, insert the hook between the stems of the stitches, not under the plaited top. Make sure to count the stitches at the end of your round.*

 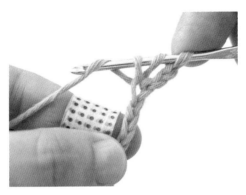 

DOUBLE CROCHET (abbreviation: dc)

Probably the best-known crochet stitch to crochet garments and blankets. We only use it sporadically when crocheting toys.

In rows (flat fabric)

Start from a foundation chain. The first three chain stitches of the foundation chain are the turning chain for the first row.

1 Yarn over. Insert the hook into the fourth chain from the hook and yarn over again. Draw the yarn through the loop. You now have three loops on the hook.

2 Yarn over again and draw through the first two loops on the hook.

3 You now have two loops on the hook. Wrap the yarn over the hook one last time and draw it through both loops on the hook.

4 You have now completed one double crochet stitch.

5 Yarn over and insert the hook into the next stitch. Continue crocheting into every chain stitch. At the end of the row, make three turning chains and turn the work horizontally to begin the next row.

6 Crochet one double crochet stitch into the fourth stitch from the hook, inserting the hook under both loops of the stitch in the row below. Repeat until you reach the end of the row.

BOBBLE STITCH *(abbreviation: 5-dc-bobble)*

A bobble stitch is a cluster of double crochet stitches worked into one stitch, joined by leaving the last loop of each stitch temporarily on the hook until they are closed together at the end. I use this stitch on many of my toys to make fingers and toes.

1 Yarn over. Insert the hook into the next stitch.
2 Yarn over again and draw the yarn through the stitch. You now have three loops on the hook.
3 Yarn over the hook again and draw it through the first two loops on the hook. You now have one half-closed double crochet stitch, and two loops remaining on the hook.
4 In the same stitch, repeat the preceding steps four times. You now have 5 half-closed double crochet stitches into one stitch.
5 Yarn over and draw through all six loops on the hook at once. You have now completed one 5-dc bobble stitch.

MOSS STITCH

This is my favorite stitch when making blankets. It looks a bit like knitwork, it's fast and easy to crochet and gives you the loose and fluid finish of the half double crochet, all while using less yarn.

In rows (flat fabric)

Start from a foundation chain with an even number of chains.
1 Sc in the 4th chain from hook, (ch 1, skip 1 ch, sc in next ch) repeat to the end. The last stitch should be a single crochet stitch. Ch 2, turn.
2 Sc in next ch-1 space, (ch 1, sc in next ch-1 space) repeat to the end. Finish with a sc in the ch-3 space at the start of the first row. Ch 2, turn.
3 Sc in next ch-1 space, (ch 1, sc in next ch-1 space) repeat to the end. Finish with a sc in the ch-2 space at the start of the previous row. Ch 2, turn.
Repeat row 3 until you reach your desired length.

MOSS STITCH

BASKET SPIKE STITCH

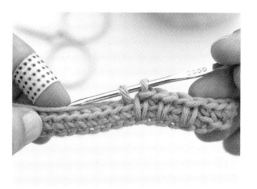

BASKET SPIKE STITCH

This stitch is named for its basket-rattan look. I've only worked it in the round because it doesn't look so neat when crocheted in rows. Alternate one spike single crochet with a regular BLO single crochet to get the desired effect. For this stitch, I use the V-shaped single crochet in order to obtain two straight vertical lines.

Spike single crochet (spike)

Place your hook in the next stitch one round below (into the same place where that stitch was worked). Yarn over and draw up a loop of yarn up to the height of the actual round. Draw the yarn through both loops on your hook.

In a spiral (a tube)

Start from a foundation chain. Make sure your chain isn't twisted and put the hook through the first chain stitch. Close into a ring by making one slip stitch in the first chain. Continue crocheting one single crochet into each chain stitch until you reach the beginning.

1-2 (BLO sc in next st, spike in next st of the previous round repeat until the end of the round.

3-4 (spike in next st of the previous round, BLO sc in next st) repeat until the end of the round.

Repeat until you get the number of rounds needed.

SINGLE RIB CROCHET (POST OR RELIEF STITCH)

I use this method to make ribbings of hats and other garments. This technique is more common with double crochet, but it works fine with single crochet as well. It's made by alternating one front post and one back post stitch. You should have at least one row or round of single crochet stitches before beginning these raised stitches.

1-2 Insert the hook from front to back to front around the post of the single crochet stitch from the previous round or row. Yarn over and pull a loop around the post. Pull out a little more yarn than for a standard single crochet stitch. Yarn over and draw through the two loops on the hook. You have now finished your first front post stitch.

3-4 Insert the hook from back to front to back around the post of the next single crochet stitch. Yarn over and pull a loop around the post. Pull out a little more yarn than for a normal single crochet stitch. Yarn over and draw through the two loops on the hook. You have now finished your first back post stitch.

5-6 Repeat steps 1-4 until the end of the round or row.

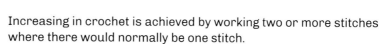

INCREASES AND DECREASES

Increases and decreases are used for shaping any crochet garment or object.

Increase (*abbreviation: inc*)

Increasing in crochet is achieved by working two or more stitches where there would normally be one stitch.

1   Work a stitch into the next stitch of the previous row or round.
2   Insert your hook in exactly the same stitch and pull up a loop.
3   Work a second stitch.

Decrease (*abbreviation: dec*)

Decreasing is achieved by crocheting two or more stitches together. There are a couple of methods, but for my toys I always use the "traditional decrease" because it's the method I learned first and it comes naturally to me. Nowadays, it's become less popular because it can leave a small gap if not tightened properly.

1-2   Work two incomplete stitches in two adjacent stitches on the previous round or row.
3   Yarn over.
4   Pull the loop through all three loops on the hook.

Working in spirals

Increasing stitches from the center out is a technique used to make round pieces, such as hats and doilies. When crocheting in rounds, we traditionally close each round with a slip stitch. This technique, despite generating perfect circles, leaves a continuous mark as the result of joining rounds, something like a scar, and it's not pretty at all on a cute toy.

To avoid this mark, we usually choose to crochet in spirals, that is, without closing the rounds.

When working in continuous spirals, it's highly recommended to use a stitch marker. This tool will show you where a new round begins and the previous one ended. You can choose to place it at the end or the beginning of each round (be consistent in what you choose). After crocheting the round, you should end up right above your stitch marker. Move it at the beginning or the end of each round to keep track of where you are.

MAGIC RING

This is, almost without a doubt, the best way to start crocheting in the round. You start by working the required number of stitches on an adjustable loop and then pull the loop tight until the stitches are closed in a ring.

There are several techniques to start the magic ring, and all of them may seem a bit scary at first. Practice, practice and don't worry if it appears impossible during the first attempts. I can assure you that once you've finished your first toy, you will have mastered this technique. And you'll love it!

1 Start with the yarn crossed to form a circle, as if you were to start a slip knot.

2-3 Holding the loop tight between your thumb and index finger, insert the hook in the middle of the circle and draw up a loop.

4 Keep holding the ring tight (this is crucial!) and yarn over again. Pull the yarn through the loop on your hook to make a chain stitch. This chain stitch will secure the ring.

5-6 Insert the hook again into the loop and underneath the tail (they look like two strands crossed). Yarn over the hook and draw up a loop.

7 Yarn over again. Draw the loop through both loops on the hook. You've now made your first single crochet in the ring.

8 Make as many stitches as required in the pattern. Grab the yarn tail and pull to draw the center of the ring tightly closed. Don't be afraid to pull it really tight.

9 You can opt to join the circle with a slip stitch, but this is not necessary. It's the only point where I myself join the rounds.

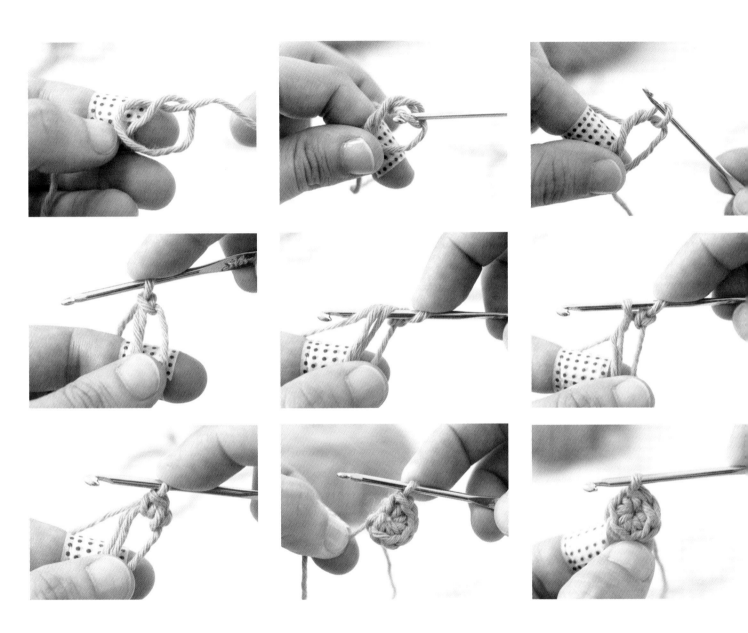

CROCHETING AROUND A FOUNDATION CHAIN

When you want to start an oval piece instead of a circle, you can start by working around a foundation chain. It's the traditional method to start rugs or bags and, in case of toys, we'll be using this technique for crocheting snouts, ears and the body of some characters.

1   Work a foundation chain with as many stitches as required. Start in the second chain from the hook and make a single crochet stitch (sometimes, the pattern may require an increase stitch).

Continue crocheting single crochet stitches into each chain stitch.

2   The last stitch is usually an increase stitch, so we can turn the work and continue working on the other side of the foundation chain.

3-4   Turn your work upside down to work into the underside of the stitches. Notice that only one loop is available.

5   Continue crocheting into each loop across. Your last single crochet stitch should be next to the first stitch you made. It can also be an increase stitch (depending on the pattern).

6   You can now continue working in spirals.

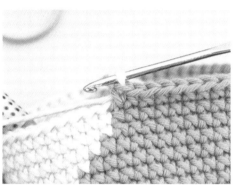

CHANGING COLOR AND JOINING YARN

Use this technique when you want to switch from one color to the next or join yarn because you ran out of the one you were crocheting with.

1 Work in the previous color (or yarn) until two loops of the last stitch remain on the hook.
2 Use the new color (or yarn) to complete the stitch. Continue working with the new color (or yarn) as before. Try not to cut off any yarn tails that will be needed later on. I knot both yarns, to make sure the stitch stays tight.

Note: *If you are working stripes of different colors in rows, make the color change in the last stitch of the previous row.*

TAPESTRY CROCHET
IN BOTH LOOPS

TAPESTRY CROCHET
IN FLO

TAPESTRY CROCHET
IN BLO

JACQUARD AND TAPESTRY

These two funny words come from other textile worlds, knitting and weaving, but crocheters managed to adapt these color change techniques to crochet. They are used to create motifs and patterns with two or more colors, much like drawing with different yarn colors.
It's common to work these motifs by following a diagram that shows you the color for each stitch. Using a diagram makes it easier to count stitches.

The difference between the two techniques is how the different strands of color are carried through the work.

When working **jacquard**, we leave the yarn we don't use behind the work. When it's time to use it again, you pick up the yarn and carry it across the back (inside) of your work before making the next color change.
When the pattern indicates to make a color change, it's really important to remember that the change must always be started one stitch earlier. Crochet the number of stitches as indicated by the pattern/diagram. Taking into account that the color change always starts a stitch before, take the strand of the color that you want to use and carry it from behind to the place where you want to change color. The strands that remain inside your crochetwork between color changes must be loose enough so that the fabric doesn't pucker.

Note: When working jacquard with color changes that are widely spread, I like to cut the inside strands and tie them together. In fact, it is recommended if the color change causes your thread to cross the crochetwork and make a web that doesn't allow you to stuff properly. If you don't want to cut your yarn, you can also use the technique of picking up the loose strand every couple of stitches.

When working the **tapestry technique,** you carry the yarn strand along within the stitches (on top of the V) while continuing to crochet with the other color. This means that every time we make a stitch, we'll be wrapping the strand(s) of the other yarn color(s) that we aren't using. This apparently small difference with the jacquard technique will result in a significantly different fabric, especially on the backside (or "wrong" side): it results in a piece of fabric that resembles a tapestry (hence the name!) and has the great advantage that there are no loose threads on either side. Therefore, it's great to crochet garments or accessories where we want the fabric to look nice on both sides. However, the small disadvantage I do see is that, unless you carry the threads throughout the entire work, the place where you crochet using this technique results in a rather thick fabric, and the threads of the "hidden" colors can be seen between the stitches.

Note: If you want straight vertical lines using the tapestry technique with single crochet stitches, you may want to crochet FLO or BLO (sample on page 35).

FASTENING OFF

When you finish your work and want to fasten off the yarn permanently, cut the yarn about 2 inches / 5 cm away from the last stitch. Draw the end through the loop on the hook.

If you are going to sew the piece, you may have to cut the yarn much longer, depending on how many stitches you'll have to sew. If you are not going to sew this piece, or if you have finished the last round of a stuffed piece, you may want to weave in the yarn end.

Weave in the yarn end on a flat fabric

Thread the yarn end into a tapestry needle. With the wrong side facing, weave the end into a single row or several stitches, wrapping the yarn end into the loops at the bottom of the rows. You can also pass the yarn through the loops on the side. Cut the remaining tail.

Weave in the yarn end on a stuffed piece

1-2 Finish the last round of decreases and fasten off, leaving a long tail of 6 inches / 15 cm. Thread the yarn tail into a tapestry needle and, from back to front, weave it through the front loop of each remaining stitch.

3   Pull the yarn tail tight to close. Weave it through one or two more stitches to secure the tail. Trim the excess yarn and hide it into the piece with the help of your crochet hook.

EMBROIDERY

Embroidery remains a pending subject for me. I only know – more or less – how to make one embroidery stitch I learned as a child to hand-sew doll dresses: the **backstitch**. It creates a nice line made up of straight stitches.

1   Thread your tapestry needle. Insert the needle from behind your work and make a single straight stitch the same length as your single crochet stitch. I like to use the gaps between the stitches to insert and pass the tapestry needle through.
2   Continue along, as many times as you need, coming up one space ahead and bringing your needle back down into the same hole at the end of the last stitch you've made.

JOINING PARTS (SEWING)

I'm one of many crocheters who would happily pay someone to do the sewing part for me. But, as there are no volunteers (yet), we better practice a simple and satisfactory method. If you're having doubts about where to place the parts, you can pin them to see how they look and adjust if necessary. If possible, use the leftover yarn tail from where you fastened off.

Joining open pieces

Use this technique to sew snouts, cheeks, beaks, horns, etc., to an open and unstuffed piece, like a head.
Thread the tapestry needle and position the piece. Use pins if you need them! If you are sewing a snout or a beak on a face, I recommend you position it on the opposite side of where your stitch marker is located, for aesthetic reasons. This way your color changes will be at the back of your toy. Make the first stitch, inserting the needle from front to back (inside). Using backstitching, sew passing under both loops of each stitch from the final round of the piece to be attached. Go from back to front and front to back. If the piece has 30 stitches, you'll have to make at least 30 backstitches. Before getting to the end, remember to stuff the piece. I try not to stuff the pieces until the very end, to avoid the filling getting entangled in the stitches.

Joining an open end piece with a closed piece

I'll explain how to sew an open piece (with or without stuffing) onto a finished and closed part without closing the opening first. Thread the tapestry needle. Place the pieces on top of each other and try to line up the stitches of one piece with the other, if possible. Insert the needle through one loop of the closed (and stuffed) piece (for example the body). Now pass the needle under both loops of the stitch from the piece to be sewn. Sew around the whole piece and fasten off. Weave in the yarn tail.

READING A PATTERN

Crochet has its own lingo and, like all lingos, its own peculiarities. The crochet terminology not only differs between countries, it even has its local variations in the same country. The table below is a brief guide to the most commonly used stitch terms and their crochet symbols. In this book, I use US terms.

US	UK	LATIN AMERICA	SPAIN	SYMBOL
stitch (st)	stitch (st)	punto (p/pt)	punto (p/pt)	
chain (ch)	chain (ch)	cadena (c/cad)	cadeneta (c/cad)	⌒
slip stitch (slst)	slip stitch (slst)	punto corrido / pasado (pc/pp)	punto raso / enano (pr/pe)	●
single crochet (sc)	double crochet (dc)	medio punto (mp)	punto bajo (pb)	×
half double crochet (hdc)	half treble crochet (htc)	media vareta (mv/pmv)	punto (alto) medio (pm)	T
double crochet (dc)	treble crochet (tr)	vareta (v/pv)	punto alto (pa)	ꝼ
bobble stitch	bobble stitch	punto mota / piña	punto piña	⊕
increase (inc)	increase (inc)	aumento (aum)	aumento (aum)	ꝿ
decrease (dec)	decrease (dec)	disminución (dism)	disminución (dism)	ꙿ
row/round (Rnd)	row/round (Rnd)	hilera (h) / carrera vuelta / ronda (r)	hilera (h) / carrera vuelta / ronda (r)	
ring	ring	anillo	anillo	

PARENTHESES AND BRACKETS

In this book, I use parentheses (rounded brackets) to indicate the instructions that should be repeated across the round or row a required number of times. The number within square brackets at the end of each line shows the total number of stitches you should have in the previous round.
For example: **Rnd 3:** (sc in next st, inc in next st) repeat 6 times [18]
Rnd 3 indicates in which round you are. The instructions inside the parentheses are the stitches you have to work 6 times through the round. 18 is the total number of stitches you should have at the end.
When directions for one round must be repeated through several rounds, you will read "Rnd 10 – 20", which indicates that you have to follow the same instructions from round 10 up to (and including) round 20.

Logan Koala

Growing up by the beach with one echidna and two wallaby sisters, one wombat and three platypus brothers, Logan always had to work a little harder to get what he wanted ... And what he wanted, was to surf the waves like his older brothers and sisters. With only two boards for the entire family, Logan learned how to be patient. He knows how lucky he is to be loved by his family and always have someone to hug him when he's afraid or feeling a little blue. Logan is now finishing his studies in environmental engineering, it's the best way to return the love he received and take care of the home that gave him everything.

GALLERY: Scan or visit *www.amigurumi.com/3101* to share pictures and find inspiration.

Note: All parts are worked in worsted weight yarn, except those that are worked in a blend of two colors.

Note: The head and body are worked in one piece.

NOSE

(start in graphite gray)
Rnd 1: start 6 sc in a magic ring [6]
Rnd 2: inc in all 6 st [12]
Rnd 3: (sc in next st, inc in next st) repeat 6 times [18]
Rnd 4 – 8: sc in all 18 st [18]
Change to ash gray and off-white blend. Fasten off the graphite gray yarn, leaving a long tail for sewing.
Rnd 9 – 13: sc in all 18 st [18]
Embroider the mouth with black yarn. Stuff the nose lightly.
Rnd 14: (sc in next st, dec) repeat 6 times [12]
Rnd 15: dec 6 times [6]
Fasten off leaving a long tail. Using a tapestry needle, weave the yarn through the front loop of each remaining stitch and pull tight to close. Leave long tail for sewing.

HEAD AND BODY

(start in ash gray)
Rnd 1: start 6 sc in a magic ring [6]
Rnd 2: inc in all 6 st [12]
Rnd 3: (sc in next st, inc in next st) repeat 6 times [18]
Rnd 4: (sc in next 2 st, inc in next st) repeat 6 times [24]
Rnd 5: (sc in next 3 st, inc in next st) repeat 6 times [30]
Rnd 6: (sc in next 4 st, inc in next st) repeat 6 times [36]
Rnd 7: (sc in next 5 st, inc in next st) repeat 6 times [42]
Rnd 8: (sc in next 6 st, inc in next st) repeat 6 times [48]
Rnd 9: (sc in next 7 st, inc in next st) repeat 6 times [54]
Rnd 10: (sc in next 8 st, inc in next st) repeat 6 times [60]
Rnd 11 – 22: sc in all 60 st [60]
Rnd 23: (sc in next 3 st, dec) repeat 12 times [48]
Rnd 24: (sc in next 2 st, dec) repeat 12 times [36]

Sew the nose between rounds 8 and 22. Insert the safety eyes between rounds 16 and 17, about 3 stitches away from the nose. Embroider the cheeks with pastel pink yarn.

Rnd 25: (sc in next 4 st, dec) repeat 6 times [30]
Rnd 26: (sc in next 3 st, dec) repeat 6 times [24]
Rnd 27: (sc in next 4 st, dec) repeat 4 times [20]
Stuff the head firmly. Change to teal green yarn.
Rnd 28: (sc in next 4 st, inc in next st) repeat 4 times [24]
Rnd 29: (sc in next 3 st, inc in next st) repeat 6 times [30]
Rnd 30: (sc in next 4 st, inc in next st) repeat 6 times [36]
Rnd 31 – 36: sc in all 36 st [36]

Rnd 37: (sc in next 8 st, inc in next st) repeat 4 times [40]
Rnd 38: sc in all 40 st [40]
Embroider the leaf pattern on the T-shirt with green and pastel pink yarn. Change to ash gray yarn.
Rnd 39: BLO sc in all 40 st [40]
Rnd 40 – 45: sc in all 40 st [40]

LEGS

To make the legs, divide the work identifying 4 stitches for the front central space between the legs, 4 stitches for the back and 16 stitches for each leg (you may find it useful to use stitch markers). If the legs do not line up nicely with the head, crochet a few more sc on the body or undo them. Join the last stitch for the leg on the back side to the front side, working a single crochet stitch (this sc will be the first stitch of the leg). Now the stitches of the first leg are joined in the round. Continue working the first leg:
Rnd 46 – 49: sc in all 16 st [16]

Rnd 50: (sc in next 6 st, dec) repeat 2 times [14]
Rnd 51: sc in all 14 st [14]
Rnd 52: (sc in next 5 st, dec) repeat 2 times [12]
Rnd 53: sc in all 12 st [12]
Stuff the body and leg firmly.
Rnd 54: dec 6 times [6]
Fasten off, leaving a long tail. Using a tapestry needle, weave the yarn tail through the front loop of each remaining stitch and pull tight to close. Weave in the yarn end.

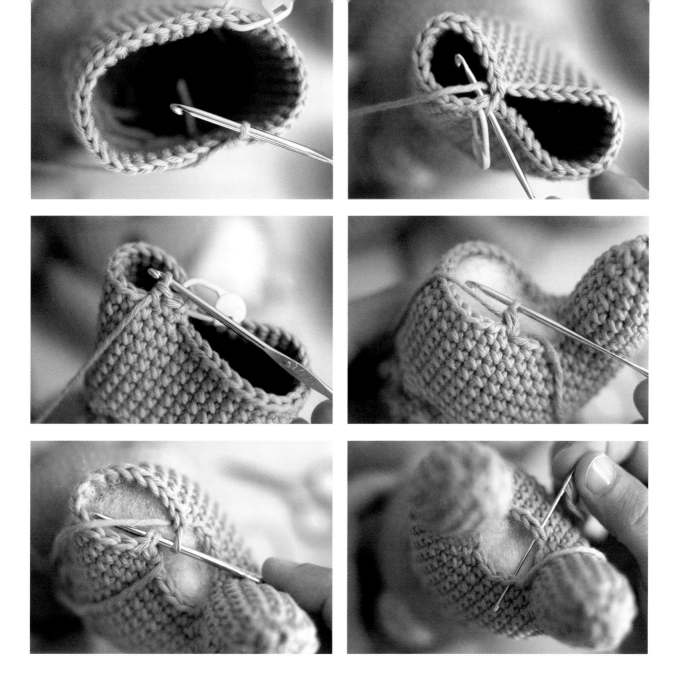

SECOND LEG

Rejoin the ash gray yarn in the fifth unworked stitch at the back of round 45. Leave a long starting yarn tail. This is where we start the first stitch of the second leg.

Rnd 46: sc in all 16 st. When you reach the 16th stitch of the leg, sc in first st to join the round [16]

Rnd 47 – 54: repeat the pattern for the first leg. Add more stuffing if needed. Using a tapestry needle, sew the 4 stitches between the legs closed.

ARMS

(make 2, start in ash gray)
Rnd 1: start 6 sc in a magic ring [6]
Rnd 2: sc in all 6 st [6]
Rnd 3: (sc in next st, inc in next st) repeat 3 times [9]
Rnd 4 – 5: sc in all 9 st [9]
Rnd 6: (sc in next 2 st, inc in next st) repeat 3 times [12]
Rnd 7 – 8: sc in all 12 st [12]
Rnd 9: (sc in next 3 st, inc in next st) repeat 3 times [15]
Rnd 10 – 12: sc in all 15 st [15]
Change to teal green yarn.
Rnd 13: sc in all 15 st [15]
Rnd 14: (sc in next 3 st, dec) repeat 3 times [12]
Rnd 15: (sc in next 4 st, dec) repeat 2 times [10]
Fasten off, leaving a long tail for sewing. Embroider the leaf pattern with green and pastel pink yarn. Stuff with fiberfill. Sew the arms to both sides between rounds 29 and 30.

EARS

(make 2, in ash gray)
Rnd 1: start 6 sc in a magic ring [6]
Rnd 2: inc in all 6 st [12]
Rnd 3: (sc in next st, inc in next st) repeat 6 times [18]
Rnd 4: (sc in next 2 st, inc in next st) repeat 6 times [24]
Rnd 5: (sc in next 3 st, inc in next st) repeat 6 times [30]
Rnd 6: (sc in next 4 st, inc in next st) repeat 6 times [36]
Rnd 7 – 12: sc in all 36 st [36]
Fasten off, leaving a long tail for sewing. Do not stuff. Flatten the ear. Make two 2 inches / 5 cm pompons with off-white yarn. Attach them to the inside of the ear. Sew the ears to the head.

48

Darwin Turtle

Darwin was born 60 years ago on the famous and beautiful Galápagos Islands. His family has lived for a long, long time and Darwin's proud to say that, in fact, his uncle was a personal friend of Charles Darwin, and even boarded the HMS Beagle for a while. When he found out about the origin of his name, Darwin decided to study natural history, at his own pace. In the meantime, he enjoys his work as a tour guide of the islands, informing tourists about all that he's learned in his courses, taking notes on all the new things he discovers on the way and, of course, telling everyone who will listen about that time when his uncle met the very same Charles Darwin.

GALLERY: Scan or visit *www.amigurumi.com/3102* to share pictures and find inspiration.

Size:
9.5 inches / 24 cm tall when made with the indicated yarn

Materials:
– Worsted weight yarn in
  · sage green
  · off-white
  · French blue
  · graphite gray
  · light aqua blue (leftover)
  · pastel pink
  · yellow
  · black (leftover)
– Size C-2 / 2.75 mm crochet hook
– Black safety eyes (10 mm)
– Fiberfill

Skills needed: magic ring *(page 32)*, working around a foundation chain *(page 34)*, changing color at the beginning of a round *(page 35)*, dividing the body in 2 parts *(page 47)*, embroidery *(page 38)*, joining parts *(page 39)*

Note: The head and body are worked in one piece.

CHEEKS

(in pastel pink)
Rnd 1: start 6 sc in a magic ring [6]
Rnd 2: inc in all 6 st [12]
Slst in next st. Fasten off, leaving a long tail for sewing.

HEAD AND BODY

(start in sage green)
Rnd 1: start 6 sc in a magic ring [6]
Rnd 2: inc in all 6 st [12]
Rnd 3: (sc in next st, inc in next st) repeat 6 times [18]
Rnd 4: (sc in next 2 st, inc in next st) repeat 6 times [24]
Rnd 5: (sc in next 3 st, inc in next st) repeat 6 times [30]
Rnd 6: (sc in next 4 st, inc in next st) repeat 6 times [36]
Rnd 7: (sc in next 5 st, inc in next st) repeat 6 times [42]
Rnd 8: (sc in next 6 st, inc in next st) repeat 6 times [48]

Rnd 9: (sc in next 7 st, inc in next st) repeat 6 times [54]
Rnd 10: (sc in next 8 st, inc in next st) repeat 6 times [60]
Rnd 11 – 20: sc in all 60 st [60]
Rnd 21: (sc in next 3 st, dec) repeat 12 times [48]
Rnd 22: (sc in next 2 st, dec) repeat 12 times [36]
Rnd 23: (sc in next 4 st, dec) repeat 6 times [30]
With black yarn, embroider the mouth between rounds 16 and 17. Embroider two short lines for the nose on round 14. Insert the safety eyes between rounds 15 and 16, with an interspace of 13 stitches and about 4 stitches away from the mouth. Sew the cheeks behind the eyes, between rounds 16 and 19. Embroider short light aqua blue lines on the head over rounds 9, 11 and 13.
Rnd 24: (sc in next 3 st, dec) repeat 6 times [24]
Rnd 25: (sc in next 4 st, dec) repeat 4 times [20]
Rnd 26: sc in all 20 st [20]
Stuff the head firmly with fiberfill. Continue in a stripe pattern, changing color every round, alternating white and French blue.
Rnd 27: (sc in next st, inc in next st) repeat 10 times [30]

Rnd 28: sc in all 30 st [30]
Rnd 29: (sc in next 4 st, inc in next st) repeat 6 times [36]
Rnd 30 – 34: sc in all 36 st [36]
Rnd 35: (sc in next 8 st, inc in next st) repeat 4 times [40]
Rnd 36 – 37: sc in all 40 st [40]
Change to sage green yarn.
Rnd 38: BLO sc in all 40 st [40]
Rnd 39 – 43: sc in all 40 st [40]
Rnd 44: (sc in next 8 st, dec) repeat 4 times [36]
Rnd 45 – 47: sc in all 36 st [36]

LEGS

To make the legs, divide the work identifying 3 stitches for the front central space between the legs, 3 stitches for the back and 15 stitches for each leg (you may find it useful to use stitch markers). If the legs do not line up nicely with the head, crochet a few more sc on the body or undo them. Join the last stitch for the leg on the back side to the front side, working a single crochet stitch (this sc will be the first stitch of the leg). Now the stitches of the first leg are joined in the round. Continue working the first leg:
Rnd 48 – 57: sc in all 15 st [15]
Stuff the body and leg firmly.
Rnd 58: (sc in next st, dec) repeat 5 times [10]
Rnd 59: dec 5 times [5]
Fasten off, leaving a long tail. Using a tapestry needle, weave the yarn tail through the front loop of each remaining stitch and pull tight to close. Weave in the yarn end.

SECOND LEG
Rejoin the sage green yarn in the fourth unworked stitch at the back of round 47. This is where we start the first stitch of the second leg. Leave a long starting yarn tail.
Rnd 48: sc in all 15 st. When you reach the 15th stitch of the leg, sc in first st to join the round [15]
Rnd 49 – 59: repeat the pattern for the first leg. Add more stuffing if needed. Using a tapestry needle, sew the 3 stitches between the legs closed.

LITTLE SPOTS

(make 12, in pastel pink)
Rnd 1: start 6 sc in a magic ring [6]
Slst in next st. Fasten off, leaving a long tail for sewing.

SHELL

(in graphite gray)
Rnd 1: start 6 sc in a magic ring [6]
Rnd 2: inc in all 6 st [12]
Rnd 3: (sc in next st, inc in next st) repeat 6 times [18]
Rnd 4: (sc in next st, inc in next st) repeat 9 times [27]
Rnd 5: (sc in next 2 st, inc in next st) repeat 9 times [36]
Rnd 6: (sc in next 3 st, inc in next st) repeat 9 times [45]
Rnd 7 – 8: sc in all 45 st [45]
Rnd 9: (sc in next 4 st, inc in next st) repeat 9 times [54]
Rnd 10 – 11: sc in all 54 st [54]
Rnd 12: (sc in next 5 st, inc in next st) repeat 9 times [63]
Rnd 13: sc in all 63 st [63]
Rnd 14: BLO (sc in next 5 st, dec) repeat 9 times [54]
Rnd 15: (sc in next 4 st, dec) repeat 9 times [45]
Rnd 16: (sc in next 3 st, dec) repeat 9 times [36]
Fasten off, leaving a long tail for sewing. Join the graphite gray yarn in the first front loop stitch of round 14 and FLO slst in all 63 st. Fasten off and weave in the yarn ends. Sew the little pink spots on the shell. Stuff it with fiberfill. Sew the shell between rounds 27 and 40 of the body.

ARMS

(make 2, start in sage green)
Rnd 1: start 5 sc in a magic ring [5]
Rnd 2: inc in all 5 st [10]
Rnd 3 – 12: sc in all 10 st [10]
Continue in a stripe pattern, changing color every round, alternating white and French blue yarn.
Rnd 13 – 16: sc in all 10 st [10]
Rnd 17: (sc in next 3 st, dec) repeat 2 times [8]
Fasten off, leaving a long tail for sewing. Stuff with fiberfill. Sew the arms on both sides between rounds 28 and 29.

TAIL

(in sage green)
Rnd 1: start 5 sc in a magic ring [5]
Rnd 2: sc in all 5 st [5]
Rnd 3: inc in all 5 st [10]
Fasten off, leaving a long tail for sewing. The tail does not need to be stuffed. Sew the tail to the body between rounds 41 and 42, centered below the shell.

RAIN BOOTS

(make 2, in yellow)
Ch 8. Stitches are worked around both sides of the foundation chain.
Rnd 1: start in second ch from the hook, inc in this st, sc in next 5 st, 4 sc in last st. Continue on the other side of the foundation chain, sc in next 5 st, inc in last st [18]
Rnd 2: inc in next 2 st, sc in next 5 st, inc in next 4 st, sc in next 5 st, inc in next 2 st [26]
Rnd 3: inc in next 2 st, sc in next 10 st, inc in next st, sc in next st, inc in next st, sc in next 10 st, inc in next st [31]
Rnd 4: BLO sc in all 31 st [31]
Rnd 5: sc in next 11 st, dec 2 times, sc in next st, dec 2 times, sc in next 11 st [27]
Rnd 6: sc in next 10 st, dec 5 times, sc in next 7 st [22]
Rnd 7: sc in next 10 st, dec 2 times, sc in next 8 st [20]
Rnd 8 – 10: sc in all 20 st [20]
Rnd 11: slst in all 20 st [20]
Fasten off and weave in the yarn end. Join the off-white yarn in the last front loop stitch of round 4 and FLO slst in all 31 st. Fasten off and weave in the yarn end.

Satsuki Cat

When she was just a little kitten, Satsuki received her first notebook and a 48-colors pencil case. She was so awed, that she didn't touch her gifts for days. When she did use them for the very first time, she took care not to spoil a single sheet or break a single pen. Satsuki enjoyed writing and drawing, but she liked looking at her beautiful blue-lined notebook and dazzling red pencil case even more. Over the years, she put together a stationery collection so big it took over her entire room. And when her room didn't have any more space left, she took a big leap. Today, she's the proud and happy owner of a cute little stationery shop, where she can pass on her passion to anyone entering through the red door with the blue linen curtains.

 GALLERY: Scan or visit www.amigurumi.com/3103 to share pictures and find inspiration.

Size:
12.5 inches / 31 cm tall when made with the indicated yarn

Materials:
– Worsted weight yarn in
  · ash gray
  · graphite gray
  · off-white
  · black (leftover)
  · pastel pink
  · brown
– Size C-2 / 2.75 mm crochet hook
– Black safety eyes (10 mm)
– Fiberfill

Skills needed: magic ring (page 32), working around a foundation chain (page 34), changing color at the beginning of a round (page 35), changing color mid-round (page 35), working in rows, dividing the body in 2 parts (page 47), basket spike stitch (page 29), moss stitch (page 28), embroidery (page 38), joining parts (page 39)

Note: The head and body are worked in one piece.

CHEEKS

(make 2, in pastel pink)
Rnd 1: start 8 sc in a magic ring [8]
Slst in next st. Fasten off, leaving a long tail for sewing.

MUZZLE

(in off-white)
Ch 6. Stitches are worked around both sides of the foundation chain.
Rnd 1: start in second ch from the hook, sc in next 4 st, 3 sc in last st. Continue on the other side of the foundation chain, sc in next 3 st, inc in last st [12]
Rnd 2: inc in next st, sc in next 3 st, inc in next 3 st, sc in next 3 st, inc in next 2 st [18]
Rnd 3 – 4: sc in all 18 st [18]
Fasten off, leaving a long tail for sewing. Embroider a mouth and nose with black yarn. Stuff the muzzle lightly with fiberfill.

HEAD AND BODY

(start in ash gray)
Rnd 1: start 6 sc in a magic ring [6]
Rnd 2: inc in all 6 st [12]
Rnd 3: (sc in next st, inc in next st) repeat 6 times [18]
Rnd 4: (sc in next 2 st, inc in next st) repeat 6 times [24]
Rnd 5: (sc in next 3 st, inc in next st) repeat 6 times [30]
Rnd 6: (sc in next 4 st, inc in next st) repeat 6 times [36]
Rnd 7: (sc in next 5 st, inc in next st) repeat 6 times [42]
Rnd 8: (sc in next 6 st, inc in next st) repeat 6 times [48]
Rnd 9: (sc in next 7 st, inc in next st) repeat 6 times [54]
Rnd 10 – 12: sc in all 54 st [54]
Continue working with alternating yarns (ash gray and off-white). The color you work with is indicated before each part.
Rnd 13 – 14: *(ash gray)* sc in next 26 st, *(off-white)* sc in next 2 st, *(ash gray)* sc in next 26 st [54]
Rnd 15 – 16: *(ash gray)* sc in next 25 st, *(off-white)* sc in next 4 st, *(ash gray)* sc in next 25 st [54]
Rnd 17: *(ash gray)* sc in next 24 st,

(off-white) sc in next 6 st, (ash gray) sc in next 24 st [54]

Rnd 18: (ash gray) (sc in next 2 st, inc in next st) repeat 7 times, sc in next 2 st, (off-white) (inc in next st, sc in next 2 st) repeat 3 times, (ash gray) inc in next st, (sc in next 2 st, inc in next st) repeat 7 times [72]

Continue in off-white yarn.

Rnd 19 – 21: sc in all 72 st [72]

Rnd 22: (sc in next 4 st, dec) repeat 12 times [60]

Rnd 23: (sc in next 3 st, dec) repeat 12 times [48]

Rnd 24: (sc in next 2 st, dec) repeat 12 times [36]

Sew the muzzle between rounds 17 and 22. Insert the safety eyes between rounds 17 and 18, about 2 stitches away from the muzzle. Sew the cheeks below the safety eyes. Embroider 3 horizontal lines on both sides of the head and vertical lines above the nose with graphite gray yarn.

Rnd 25: (sc in next 4 st, dec) repeat 6 times [30]

Rnd 26: (sc in next 3 st, dec) repeat 6 times [24]

Rnd 27: (sc in next 2 st, dec) repeat 6 times [18]

Rnd 28: sc in all 18 st [18]

Stuff the head firmly with fiberfill. Continue in a stripe pattern, changing color every round, alternating graphite gray and white yarn.

Rnd 29: (sc in next 2 st, inc in next st) repeat 6 times [24]

Rnd 30: (sc in next 3 st, inc in next st) repeat 6 times [30]

Rnd 31 – 33: sc in all 30 st [30]

Rnd 34: (sc in next 4 st, inc in next st) repeat 6 times [36]

Rnd 35 – 38: sc in all 36 st [36]

Change to ash gray yarn.

Rnd 39: BLO sc in all 36 st [36]

Rnd 40 – 44: sc in all 36 st [36]

LEGS

To make the legs, divide the work, identifying 3 stitches for the front central space between the legs, 3 stitches for the back and 15 stitches for each leg (you may find it useful to use stitch markers). If the legs do not line up nicely with the head, crochet a few more sc on the body or undo them. Join the last stitch for the leg on the back side to the front side, working a single crochet stitch (this sc will be the first stitch of the leg). Now the stitches of the first leg are joined in the round. Continue working the first leg:

Rnd 45 – 68: sc in all 15 st [15]

Stuff the body and leg firmly.

Rnd 69: (sc in next st, dec) repeat 5 times [10]

Rnd 70: dec 5 times [5]

Fasten off, leaving a long tail. Using a tapestry needle, weave the yarn tail through the front loop of each remaining stitch and pull tight to close. Weave in the yarn ends.

Second leg

Rejoin the ash gray yarn to the fourth unworked stitch at the back of round 44. Leave a long starting yarn tail. This is where we start the second leg.

Rnd 45: sc in next 15 st. When you reach the 15th stitch of the leg, sc in first stitch to join into the round [15]

Rnd 46 – 70: Repeat the pattern for the first leg. Add more stuffing to the body if needed. Using a tapestry needle, sew the 3 stitches between the legs closed.

ARMS

(make 2, start in ash gray)
Rnd 1: start 6 sc in a magic ring [6]
Rnd 2: inc in all 6 st [12]
Rnd 3 – 4: sc in all 12 st [12]
Rnd 5: sc in next st, 5-dc-bobble in next st, sc in next 10 st [12]
Rnd 6 – 12: sc in all 12 st [12]
Continue in a stripe pattern, changing color every round, alternating white and graphite gray yarn.
Rnd 13 – 20: sc in all 12 st [12]
Rnd 21: (sc in next st, dec) repeat 4 times [8]
Fasten off, leaving a long tail for sewing. Stuff with fiberfill. Sew the arms on both sides between rounds 30 and 31.

EARS

(make 2, in ash gray)
Rnd 1: start 5 sc in a magic ring [5]
Rnd 2: sc in all 5 st [5]
Rnd 3: inc in all 5 st [10]
Rnd 4: sc in all 10 st [10]
Rnd 5: (sc in next st, inc in next st) repeat 5 times [15]
Rnd 6: sc in all 15 st [15]
Rnd 7: (sc in next 2 st, inc in next st) repeat 5 times [20]
Rnd 8: sc in all 20 st [20]
Fasten off, leaving a long tail for sewing. Embroider pastel pink stripes on the ear. Flatten them before sewing. Do not stuff. Sew the ears to the head between rounds 3 and 12.

TAIL

(start in off-white)
Rnd 1: start 6 sc in a magic ring [6]
Rnd 2: (sc in next st, inc in next st) repeat 3 times [9]
Rnd 3 – 10: sc in all 9 st [9]
Change to ash gray yarn. Stuff lightly with fiberfill and continue stuffing as you go.
Rnd 11 – 40: sc in all 9 st [9]
Fasten off, leaving a long tail for sewing. Add more stuffing to the tail if needed. Sew the tail to the back, centered over round 41.

JUMPER DRESS

(in brown)
Ch 40. Make sure your chain isn't twisted. Insert the hook in the first chain stitch and join the foundation chain with a slst. Continue working in a spiral.
Rnd 1 – 2: sc in all 40 st [40]
Rnd 3: (sc in next 9 st, inc in next st) repeat 4 times [44]
Rnd 4: sc in all 44 st [44]
Rnd 5: (sc in next 10 st, inc in next st) repeat 4 times [48]
Rnd 6: sc in all 48 st [48]
Rnd 7: (sc in next 11 st, inc in next st) repeat 4 times [52]
Rnd 8 – 9: sc in all 52 st [52]
Rnd 10: (sc in next 12 st, inc in next st) repeat 4 times [56]
Rnd 11 – 12: sc in all 56 st [56]
Rnd 13: (sc in next 13 st, inc in next st) repeat 4 times [60]
Rnd 14 – 15: sc in all 60 st [60]
Rnd 16: (sc in next 14 st, inc in next st) repeat 4 times [64]
Rnd 17: slst in all 64 st [64]
Fasten off and weave in the yarn ends. Continue working the front bib. Work in rows on the center 8 stitches of Rnd 1. Insert your hook with the right side facing you and draw up a loop.
Row 1: sc in next 8 st, ch 2, turn [8]
Row 2: moss st in all 8 st, ch 1, turn [8]
Row 3: moss st in all 8 st [8]
Do not fasten off. Make the shoulder straps and waist-band: Ch 31, start in second ch from the hook, slst in next 30 ch, sc in next 3 row-ends on the left side of the front bib, sc in next 32 st on the waistband, sc in next 3 row-ends on the right side of the front bib. Ch 31, start in second ch from the hook, slst in next 30 ch, slst in next 6 st on the top side of the front bib.
Fasten off and weave in the yarn ends. Cross the shoulder straps at the back and sew them to the dress with an interspace of 8 stitches. Alternatively, you could tie the straps around the neck.

BOW TIE

(start in pastel pink)
Ch 35. Make sure your chain isn't twisted. Insert the hook in the first chain stitch and join the foundation chain with a slst. Continue working in a spiral.
Rnd 1: sc in next 35 st [35]
Change to off-white yarn.
Rnd 2: (BLO sc in next st, spike in the st of the previous round) repeat until the end of the round [35]
Change to pastel pink yarn.
Rnd 3: (spike in the st of the previous round, BLO sc in next st) repeat until the end of the round [35]
Rnd 4: (BLO sc in next st, spike in the st of the previous round) repeat until the end of the round [35]
Change to off-white yarn.
Rnd 5: (spike in the st of the previous round, BLO sc in next st) repeat until the end of the round [35]
Change to pastel pink yarn.
Rnd 6 – 8: repeat rounds 3 to 5.
Change to pastel pink yarn.
Rnd 9: (spike in the st of the previous round, BLO sc in next st) repeat until the end of the round [35]
Fasten off and weave in the yarn ends.

MIDDLE RIBBON
(in pastel pink)
Ch 14. Do not join. Crochet in rows.
Row 1: start in second ch from the hook, sc in next 13 st [13]
Fasten off, leaving a long tail for sewing. Pinch the bow tie together and sew the middle ribbon around the middle of the bow tie. Sew the bow tie to one of the shoulder straps.

Mario Raccoon

Mario is a bus driver and he adores his job. Five days a week, he drives his bus through the valley, connecting two little towns and passing through a small village by the river. Mario enjoys watching the seasons change (he's also a poet at heart), but what he cherishes the most, are the chats with his passengers. Mario loves talking about the weather or the next harvest and, you know, sharing a bit of gossip. After reading a column on the life of famous authors, Mario came up with the idea of writing down the stories of all the people he had driven around throughout the years. He now takes advantage of his two-hour break to write down ideas. He already has enough material to write a 3-volume saga, but he says he still needs more (though that might be an excuse to gossip even more).

GALLERY: Scan or visit www.amigurumi.com/3104 to share pictures and find inspiration.

Size:
9.5 inches / 24 cm tall when made with the indicated yarn

Materials:
– Worsted weight yarn in
  · light warm gray
  · dark warm gray
  · greenish gray
  · mustard
  · off-white (leftover)
  · black (leftover)
  · pastel pink (leftover)
– Size C-2 / 2.75 mm crochet hook
– Size E-4 / 3.5 mm crochet hook
– Black safety eyes (10 mm)
– Fiberfill

Skills needed: magic ring (page 32), changing color at the beginning of a round (page 35), changing color mid-round (page 35), working in rows, dividing the body in 2 parts (page 47), single rib crochet (page 30), embroidery (page 38), joining parts (page 39)

Note: Use a size C-2 / 2.75 mm crochet hook, unless otherwise noted.

Note: The head and body are worked in one piece.

SNOUT

(start in black)
Rnd 1: start 6 sc in a magic ring [6]
Rnd 2: inc in all 6 st [12]
Rnd 3: sc in all 12 st [12]
Continue working with alternating yarns (off-white and dark warm gray). The color you work with is indicated before each part.
Rnd 4: *(off-white)* sc in next 4 st, *(dark warm gray)* sc in next 4 st, *(off-white)* sc in next 4 st [12]
Rnd 5: *(off-white)* (sc in next st, inc in next st) repeat 2 times, *(dark warm gray)* (sc in next st, inc in next st) repeat 2 times, *(off-white)* (sc in next st, inc in next st) repeat 2 times [18]
Rnd 6 – 8: *(off-white)* sc in next 6 st, *(dark warm gray)* sc in next 6 st, *(off-white)* sc in next 6 st [18]
Fasten off, leaving a long tail for sewing. Embroider the mouth with black yarn. Stuff the snout with fiberfill.

HEAD AND BODY

(start in light warm gray)
Rnd 1: start 6 sc in a magic ring [6]
Rnd 2: inc in all 6 st [12]
Rnd 3: (sc in next st, inc in next st) repeat 6 times [18]
Rnd 4: (sc in next st, inc in next st) repeat 9 times [27]
Rnd 5: (sc in next 2 st, inc in next st) repeat 9 times [36]
Rnd 6: (sc in next 3 st, inc in next st) repeat 9 times [45]
Rnd 7: (sc in next 4 st, inc in next st) repeat 9 times [54]
Rnd 8 – 10: sc in all 54 st [54]
Rnd 11: (sc in next 8 st, inc in next st) repeat 6 times [60]
Continue working with alternating yarns (light warm gray, off-white and dark warm gray). The color you work with is indicated before each part.
Rnd 12: *(light warm gray)* sc in next 19 st, *(off-white)* sc in next 22 st, *(light warm gray)* sc in next 19 st [60]
Rnd 13: *(light warm gray)* sc in next 17 st, *(off-white)* sc in next 2 st, *(dark warm gray)* sc in next 22 st, *(off-white)* sc in next 2 st, *(light warm gray)* sc in next 17 st [60]

Rnd 14: (light warm gray) sc in next 16 st, (off-white) sc in next 2 st, (dark warm gray) sc in next 24 st, (off-white) sc in next 2 st, (light warm gray) sc in next 16 st [60]

Fasten off the off-white yarn, continue in light warm gray and dark warm gray.

Rnd 15: (light warm gray) sc in next 9 st, inc in next st, sc in next 6 st, (dark warm gray) sc in next 3 st, inc in next st, (sc in next 9 st, inc in next st) repeat 2 times, sc in next 4 st, (light warm gray) sc in next 5 st, inc in next st, sc in next 9 st, inc in next st [66]

Rnd 16 – 18: (light warm gray) sc in next 17 st, (dark warm gray) sc in next 31 st, (light warm gray) sc in next 18 st [66]

Rnd 19: (light warm gray) sc in next 19 st, (dark warm gray) sc in next 27 st, (light warm gray) sc in next 20 st [66]

Rnd 20: (light warm gray) sc in next 9 st, dec, sc in next 9 st, (dark warm gray) dec, (sc in next 9 st, dec) repeat 2 times, sc in next st, (light warm gray) sc in next 8 st, dec, sc in next 9 st, dec [60]

Continue in light warm gray yarn.

Rnd 21: (sc in next 8 st, dec) repeat 6 times [54]

Rnd 22: (sc in next 4 st, dec) repeat 9 times [45]

Sew the snout between rounds 15 and 20. Insert the safety eyes between rounds 16 and 17, about 3 stitches away from the snout. Embroider the cheeks with pastel pink yarn.

Rnd 23: (sc in next 3 st, dec) repeat 9 times [36]

Rnd 24: (sc in next 4 st, dec) repeat 6 times [30]

Rnd 25: (sc in next 3 st, dec) repeat 6 times [24]

Rnd 26: sc in all 24 st [24]

Stuff the head with fiberfill. Change to mustard yarn.

Rnd 27: (sc in next 3 st, inc in next st) repeat 6 times [30]

Rnd 28: sc in all 30 st [30]

Rnd 29: (sc in next 4 st, inc in next st) repeat 6 times [36]

Rnd 30 – 31: sc in all 36 st [36]

Rnd 32: (sc in next 5 st, inc in next st) repeat 6 times [42]

Rnd 33 – 36: sc in all 42 st [42]

Rnd 37: (sc in next 6 st, inc in next st) repeat 6 times [48]

Rnd 38 – 39: sc in all 48 st [48]

Change to light warm gray yarn.

Rnd 40: BLO sc in all 48 st [48]

Rnd 41 – 47: sc in all 48 st [48]

Rnd 48: (sc in next 6 st, dec) repeat 6 times [42]

Rnd 49 – 51: sc in all 42 st [42]

LEGS

To make the legs, divide the work identifying 5 stitches for the front central space between the legs, 5 stitches for the back and 16 stitches for each leg (you may find it useful to use stitch markers). If the legs do not line up nicely with the head, crochet a few more sc on the body or undo them. Join the last stitch for the leg on the back side to the front side, working a single crochet stitch (this sc will be the first stitch of the leg). Now the stitches of the first leg are joined in the round. Continue working the first leg:

Rnd 52 – 54: sc in all 16 st [16]

Change to dark warm gray yarn.

Rnd 55: BLO (sc in next 2 st, dec) repeat 4 times [12]

Rnd 56 – 60: sc in all 12 st [12]

Stuff the body and leg firmly.

Rnd 61: dec 6 times [6]

Fasten off, leaving a long tail. Using a tapestry needle, weave the yarn tail through the front loop of each remaining stitch and pull tight to close. Weave in the yarn end.

SECOND LEG

Rejoin the light warm gray yarn in the sixth unworked stitch at the back of round 51. Leave a long starting yarn tail. This is where we start the first stitch of the second leg.

Rnd 52: sc in all 16 st. When you reach the 16th st of the leg, sc in first stitch to join the round [16]

Rnd 53 – 61: repeat the pattern for the first leg. Stuff the second leg and add more stuffing to the body if needed. Using a tapestry needle, sew the 5 stitches between the legs closed.

ARMS

(make 2, start in light warm gray)
Rnd 1: start 6 sc in a magic ring [6]
Rnd 2: sc in all 6 st [6]
Rnd 3: (sc in next st, inc in next st) repeat 3 times [9]
Rnd 4 – 5: sc in all 9 st [9]
Rnd 6: (sc in next 2 st, inc in next st) repeat 3 times [12]
Rnd 7 – 12: sc in all 12 st [12]
Change to mustard yarn.
Rnd 13 – 16: sc in all 12 st [12]
Rnd 17: (sc in next 4 st, dec) repeat 2 times [10]
Fasten off, leaving a long tail for sewing. Stuff with fiberfill.
Sew the arms on both sides between rounds 28 and 29.

EARS

(make 2, start in light warm gray)
Rnd 1: start 6 sc in a magic ring [6]
Rnd 2: inc in all 6 st [12]
Continue working with alternating yarns (light warm gray and dark warm gray). The color you work with is indicated before each part.
Rnd 3: *(light warm gray)* sc in next 2 st, *(dark warm gray)* sc in next 2 st, *(light warm gray)* sc in next 8 st [12]
Rnd 4 – 6: *(light warm gray)* sc in next st, *(dark warm gray)* sc in next 4 st, *(light warm gray)* sc in next 7 st [12]
Fasten off, leaving a long tail for sewing. Do not stuff. Flatten the ears and sew them to the head.

TAIL

(start in dark warm gray)
Rnd 1: start 6 sc in a magic ring [6]
Rnd 2: inc in all 6 st [12]
Rnd 3: (sc in next st, inc in next st) repeat 6 times [18]
Rnd 4: (sc in next 2 st, inc in next st) repeat 6 times [24]
Rnd 5: (sc in next 3 st, inc in next st) repeat 6 times [30]
Rnd 6: (sc in next 4 st, inc in next st) repeat 6 times [36]
Rnd 7 – 8: sc in all 36 st [36]
Continue working in a stripe pattern, alternating 3 rounds in light warm gray and 3 rounds in dark warm gray yarn.
Rnd 9 – 11: sc in all 36 st [36]

Rnd 12: (sc in next 7 st, dec) repeat 4 times [32]
Rnd 13 – 14: sc in all 32 st [32]
Rnd 15: (sc in next 6 st, dec) repeat 4 times [28]
Rnd 16 – 17: sc in all 28 st [28]
Rnd 18: (sc in next 5 st, dec) repeat 4 times [24]
Rnd 19 – 20: sc in all 24 st [24]
Rnd 21: (sc in next 4 st, dec) repeat 4 times [20]
Rnd 22 – 23: sc in all 20 st [20]
Rnd 24: (sc in next 3 st, dec) repeat 4 times [16]
Rnd 25 – 26: sc in all 16 st [16]
Fasten off, leaving a long tail for sewing. Stuff with fiberfill. Sew the tail to the back, centered between rounds 43 and 46.

VEST

(in greenish gray, using a size E-4/3.5 mm crochet hook)
Ch 25. Crochet in rows.
Row 1: start in second ch from the hook, sc in next 24 st, ch 2, turn [24]
Row 2: (hdc in next 3 st, hdc inc in next st) repeat 6 times, ch 2, turn [30]
Row 3: (hdc in next 4 st, hdc inc in next st) repeat 6 times, ch 2, turn [36]
Row 4: hdc in next 5 st, ch 5, skip next 7 st, hdc in next 12 st, ch 5, skip next 7 st, hdc in next 5 st, ch 2, turn [32]
Row 5: hdc in next 32 st, ch 2, turn [32]
Row 6: (hdc in next 7 st, hdc inc in next st) repeat 4 times, ch 2, turn [36]
Row 7: hdc in next 36 st, ch 2, turn [36]
Row 8 – 9: hdc rib crochet in all 36 st [36]
Without turning, single crochet an edge all around the vest, in the row-ends up the first side, across the neck, and down the row-ends on the other side. Fasten off and weave in the yarn ends.

Agatha Bee

Agatha Bee has a large family, and she loves them and their work on the honey farm. However, since she was a teeny-tiny bee, she knew the honey business wasn't for her. She wanted to travel, but couldn't go too far (her wings are not big enough and since she was born in a marguerite field in New Zealand, she would have to cross the ocean, and that would make her seasick for sure). Luckily, on her first trip to the coast, she met some extraordinary tattoo artists and that's when she knew what she wanted to do for a living. She's working as an intern now, getting to know the craft, and ... getting tattoos all over her body. Please, don't tell her parents (though her grandpa would love her new tats).

 GALLERY: Scan or visit *www.amigurumi.com/3105* to share pictures and find inspiration.

Size:
7 inches / 18 cm tall when made with the indicated yarn

Materials:
– Worsted weight yarn in
  · ochre yellow
  · greenish gray
  · off-white
  · graphite gray
  · pastel pink
  · black (leftover)
– Size C-2 / 2.75 mm crochet hook
– Black safety eyes (oval, 12 mm)
– Fiberfill

Skills needed: magic ring *(page 32)*, working around a foundation chain *(page 34)*, changing color at the beginning of a round *(page 35)*, working jacquard crochet from a diagram *(page 36)*, embroidery *(page 38)*, joining parts *(page 39)*

Note: The head and body are worked in one piece.

CHEEKS

(in pastel pink)
Rnd 1: start 6 sc in a magic ring [6]
Slst in next st. Fasten off, leaving a long tail for sewing.

HEAD AND BODY

(start in ochre yellow)
Rnd 1: start 6 sc in a magic ring [6]
Rnd 2: inc in all 6 st [12]
Rnd 3: (sc in next st, inc in next st) repeat 6 times [18]
Rnd 4: (sc in next 2 st, inc in next st) repeat 6 times [24]
Rnd 5: (sc in next 3 st, inc in next st) repeat 6 times [30]
Rnd 6: (sc in next 4 st, inc in next st) repeat 6 times [36]
Rnd 7: (sc in next 5 st, inc in next st) repeat 6 times [42]
Rnd 8: (sc in next 6 st, inc in next st) repeat 6 times [48]

Rnd 9 – 14: sc in all 48 st [48]
Continue working in a vertical stripes pattern. The pattern is made by alternating 3 stitches in greenish gray and 3 stitches in off-white (see the diagram). In Rnd 15 the increase counts as 2 stitches. This means that sometimes the increase will be made with 2 stitches of the same color, and sometimes it will be made with one stitch in each color.
Rnd 15: (sc in next 3 st, inc in next st) repeat 12 times [60]
Rnd 16 – 19: BLO sc in all 60 st [60]
Insert the safety eyes between rounds 12 and 13, with an interspace of 10 stitches. Embroider the mouth with black yarn. Sew the cheeks next to the eyes. Continue working the dot pattern (see the diagram). Alternate 1 round in graphite gray with 1 round in a dot pattern (2 stitches in graphite gray, 1 stitch in greenish gray). The color or pattern you work with is indicated before each line.
Rnd 20: *(graphite gray)* (sc in next 3 st, dec) repeat 12 times [48]
Rnd 21: *(dot pattern)* sc in all 48 st [48]

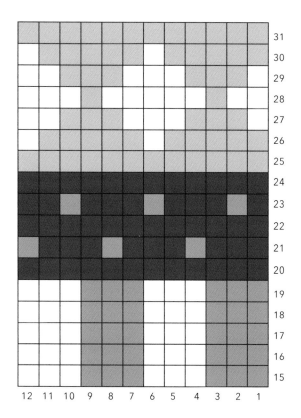

12 11 10 9 8 7 6 5 4 3 2 1

31 30 29 28 27 26 25 24 23 22 21 20 19 18 17 16 15

Rnd 22: *(graphite gray)* sc in all 48 st [48]
Rnd 23: *(begin with one stitch in graphite gray, one stitch in greenish gray and then continue in dot pattern)* sc in all 48 st [48]
Rnd 24: *(graphite gray)* sc in all 48 st [48]
Change to ochre yellow yarn. Continue in diamond pattern using ochre yellow and off-white yarn (see the diagram).
Rnd 25: (sc in next 7 st, inc in next st) repeat 6 times [54]
Rnd 26 – 31: sc in all 54 st [54]
Change to graphite gray yarn.
Rnd 32 – 33: sc in all 54 st [54]
Change to ochre yellow yarn.
Rnd 34 – 35: sc in all 54 st [54]
Rnd 36: (sc in next 7 st, dec) repeat 6 times [48]
Rnd 37: (sc in next 6 st, dec) repeat 6 times [42]
Continue in a stripe pattern, changing color every round, alternating off-white and ochre yellow yarn.

Rnd 38: sc in all 42 st [42]
Rnd 39: (sc in next 5 st, dec) repeat 6 times [36]
Rnd 40: sc in all 36 st [36]
Rnd 41: (sc in next 4 st, dec) repeat 6 times [30]
Stuff the body firmly with fiberfill.
Rnd 42: (sc in next 3 st, dec) repeat 6 times [24]
Rnd 43: (sc in next 2 st, dec) repeat 6 times [18]
Rnd 44: (sc in next st, dec) repeat 6 times [12]
Rnd 45: dec 6 times [6]
Fasten off, leaving a long tail. Add more stuffing if needed.
Using a tapestry needle, weave the yarn tail through the front loop of each remaining stitch and pull tight to close. Weave in the yarn end.

FRINGE

(in ochre yellow yarn)
Pull up a loop of ochre yellow yarn in Rnd 3 at the top of the head.
Ch 6, turn, start in second ch from the hook, slst in next 5 ch
Join with a slst in the next st to the head.
Insert the hook in the next stitch and ch 8. Turn, start in second ch from the hook, slst in next 7 ch. Join with a slst in the next st to the head.
Insert the hook in the next stitch and ch 10. Turn, start in second ch from the hook, slst in next 9 ch. Join with a slst in the next st to the head. Weave in the yarn end.

ARMS

(make 2, in graphite gray)
Rnd 1: start 7 sc in a magic ring [7]
Rnd 2 – 11: sc in all 7 st [7]
Fasten off, leaving a long tail for sewing. Stuff lightly with fiberfill.
Sew the arms on both sides between rounds 21 and 22.

LEGS

(make 2, in graphite gray)
Rnd 1: start 7 sc in a magic ring [7]
Rnd 2 – 18: sc in all 7 st [7]
Fasten off, leaving a long tail for sewing. Stuff lightly with fiberfill.
Sew the legs on both sides between rounds 35 and 36.

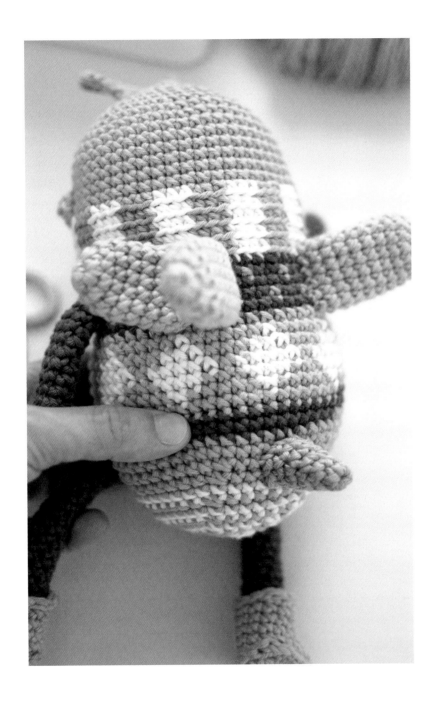

SMALL WINGS

(make 2, in pastel pink)
Rnd 1: start 6 sc in a magic ring [6]
Rnd 2: inc in all 6 st [12]
Rnd 3 – 8: sc in all 12 st [12]
Fasten off, leaving a long tail for sewing. Do not stuff. Flatten the wings before sewing. Sew the wings on the back between rounds 20 and 24, with an inter-space of 11 stitches.

BIG WINGS

(make 2, in pastel pink)
Rnd 1: start 6 sc in a magic ring [6]
Rnd 2: inc in all 6 st [12]
Rnd 3 – 10: sc in all 12 st [12]
Fasten off, leaving a long tail for sewing. Do not stuff. Flatten the wings before sewing. Sew the big wings between the small wings.

STINGER

(in greenish gray)
Rnd 1: start 6 sc in a magic ring [6]
Rnd 2: sc in all 6 st [6]
Rnd 3: (sc in next st, inc in next st) repeat 3 times [9]
Rnd 4 – 5: sc in all 9 st [9]
Fasten off, leaving a long tail for sewing. Stuff lightly with fiberfill. Sew the stinger to the back, centered over round 35.

BOOTS

(make 2, in pastel pink)
Ch 6. Stitches are worked around both sides of the foundation chain.
Rnd 1: start in second ch from the hook, inc in this st, sc in next 3 st, 4 sc in last st. Continue on the other side of the foundation chain, sc in next 3 st, inc in last st [14]
Rnd 2: inc in next 2 st, sc in next 4 st, inc in next 3 st, sc in next 4 st, inc in next st [20]
Rnd 3: BLO sc in next 9 st, dec 2 times, sc in next 7 st [18]
Rnd 4: sc in next 6 st, dec 4 times, sc in next 4 st [14]
Rnd 5: sc in next 6 st, dec 2 times, sc in next 4 st [12]
Rnd 6 – 7: sc in all 12 st [12]
Rnd 8: slst in all 12 st [12]
Fasten off and weave in the yarn end. Join the pastel pink yarn in the last front loop stitch of round 3 and FLO slst in all 20 st. Fasten off and weave in the yarn end.

Newton Owl

Newton is a cartographer. He met his best friend Darwin Turtle when mapping a group of new islands in the Pacific Ocean. Although they don't see each other a lot, they write each other the longest letters, detailing every little thing they learned while not together. Darwin can write page after page about the number of spots he saw on a ladybug, and Newton couldn't care less, but he enjoys Darwin's passion so much that he never complains, not even when he writes him for the umpteenth time about how his uncle met the very same Charles Darwin. And sometimes, these detailed descriptions come in handy, because what Newton loves doing most, is creating imaginary maps for imaginary worlds. Believe it or not, Newton is the mastermind behind the maps of many board games, stories and movies you know.

GALLERY: Scan or visit *www.amigurumi.com/3106* to share pictures and find inspiration.

SKILL LEVEL **

Size:
6.5 inches / 16 cm tall when made with the indicated yarn (ear tufts included)

Materials:
– Worsted weight yarn in
  · petrol blue
  · off-white
  · pastel pink
  · rusty red
– Size C-2 / 2.75 mm crochet hook
– Black safety eyes (oval, 12 mm)
– Fiberfill

Skills needed: magic ring *(page 32)*, changing color mid-round *(page 35)*, working jacquard crochet from a diagram *(page 36)*, embroidery *(page 38)*, joining parts *(page 39)*

Note: The head and body are worked in one piece.

Note: I made Newton's jacquard pattern crocheting under both loops. You can see how the squares tend to bend to one side. To prevent this from happening, you can work in FLO instead.

BEAK

(in rusty red)
Rnd 1: start 5 sc in a magic ring [5]
Rnd 2: sc in all 5 st [5]
Rnd 3: inc in next 5 st [10]
Fasten off, leaving a long tail for sewing. Do not stuff. Flatten the beak before sewing.

HEAD AND BODY

(start in petrol blue)
Rnd 1: start 6 sc in a magic ring [6]
Rnd 2: inc in all 6 st [12]
Rnd 3: (sc in next st, inc in next st) repeat 6 times [18]

Rnd 4: (sc in next 2 st, inc in next st) repeat 6 times [24]
Rnd 5: (sc in next 3 st, inc in next st) repeat 6 times [30]
Rnd 6: (sc in next 4 st, inc in next st) repeat 6 times [36]
Rnd 7: (sc in next 5 st, inc in next st) repeat 6 times [42]
Rnd 8: (sc in next 6 st, inc in next st) repeat 6 times [48]
Rnd 9: (sc in next 7 st, inc in next st) repeat 6 times [54]
Rnd 10: (sc in next 8 st, inc in next st) repeat 6 times [60]
Continue working with alternating yarns (petrol blue and off-white). The color you work with is indicated before each part.
Rnd 11: *(petrol blue)* sc in next 21 st, *(off-white)* sc in next 6 st, *(petrol blue)* sc in next 6 st, *(off-white)* sc in next 6 st, *(petrol blue)* sc in next 21 st [60]
Rnd 12: *(petrol blue)* sc in next 20 st, *(off-white)* sc in next 8 st, *(petrol blue)* sc in next 4 st, *(off-white)* sc in next 8 st, *(petrol blue)* sc in next 20 st [60]
Rnd 13: *(petrol blue)* sc in next 19 st, *(off-white)* sc in next 10 st, *(petrol blue)* sc in next 2 st, *(off-white)* sc in next 10 st, *(petrol blue)* sc in next 19 st [60]

Rnd 14 – 21: *(petrol blue)* sc in next 18 st, *(off-white)* sc in next 24 st, *(petrol blue)* sc in next 18 st [60]
Sew the beak between rounds 15 and 19, in the middle of the off-white patch. Insert the safety eyes between rounds 16 and 17, about 5 stitches away from the beak. Embroider the cheeks behind the eyes with pastel pink yarn.
Rnd 22: *(petrol blue)* (sc in next st, dec) repeat 6 times, *(off-white)* (sc in next st, dec) repeat 8 times, *(petrol blue)* (sc in next st, dec) repeat 6 times [40]
Rnd 23: *(petrol blue)* (sc in next 2 st, dec) repeat 3 times, *(off-white)* (sc in next 2 st, dec) repeat 4 times, *(petrol blue)* (sc in next 2 st, dec) repeat 3 times [30]
Stuff the head firmly with fiberfill. Continue in a jacquard pattern, alternating off-white, pastel pink and rusty red yarn (see the diagram).
Rnd 24: *((off-white)* sc in next 3 st, *(pastel pink)* sc in next st, inc in next st) repeat 6 times [36]
Rnd 25 – 35: sc in all 36 st [36]
Change to petrol blue yarn.
Rnd 36: sc in all 36 st [36]
Rnd 37: (sc in next 4 st, dec) repeat 6 times [30]
Rnd 38: (sc in next 3 st, dec) repeat 6 times [24]
Rnd 39: (sc in next 2 st, dec) repeat 6 times [18]
Stuff the body firmly with fiberfill.
Rnd 40: (sc in next st, dec) repeat 6 times [12]

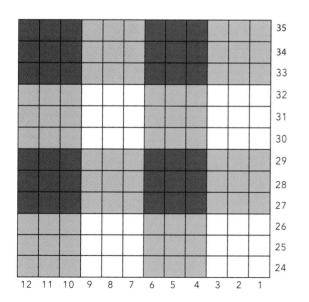

Rnd 41: dec 6 times [6]
Fasten off, leaving a long tail. Using a tapestry needle, weave the yarn tail through the front loop of each remaining stitch and pull tight to close. Weave in the yarn end.

WINGS

(make 2, in petrol blue)
Rnd 1: start 6 sc in a magic ring [6]
Rnd 2: inc in all 6 st [12]
Rnd 3: (sc in next st, inc in next st) repeat 6 times [18]
Rnd 4: (sc in next 2 st, inc in next st) repeat 6 times [24]
Rnd 5 – 10: sc in all 24 st [24]
Rnd 11: (sc in next st, inc in next st) repeat 12 times [36]
Next, we will divide the wing to make 3 feathers, using 12 stitches for each feather (see reference pictures page 96).

FIRST FEATHER
Rnd 1: sc in next 6 st and join the last stitch to the 31st stitch of the previous round with a sc stitch. This sc will be the first stitch of the next round.
Rnd 2: sc in all 12 st [12]
Rnd 3: dec 6 times [6]
Fasten off, leaving a long tail. Using a tapestry needle, weave the yarn tail through the front loop of each remaining stitch and pull tight to close. Weave in the yarn end.

SECOND FEATHER
Rejoin the petrol blue yarn to the stitch to the left of the first feather.
Rnd 1: sc in next 6 st and join the last stitch to the 6th stitch to the right side of the first feather. This sc will be the first stitch of the next round.
Rnd 2 – 3: repeat rounds 2-3 of the first feather.
Fasten off, leaving a long tail. Using a tapestry needle, weave the yarn tail through the front loop of each remaining stitch and pull tight to close. Weave in the yarn end.

THIRD FEATHER
Rejoin petrol blue yarn to the stitch to the left of the second feather.
Rnd 1 – 2: sc in all 12 st [12]
Rnd 3: dec 6 times [6]
Fasten off, leaving a long tail. Using a tapestry needle, weave the yarn tail through the front loop of each remaining stitch and pull tight to close. Weave in the yarn end. Sew the wings to the body.

EAR TUFTS

(make 4, in petrol blue)
Rnd 1: start 8 sc in a magic ring [8]
Rnd 2 – 5: sc in all 8 st [8]
Fasten off, leaving a long tail for sewing.
Do not stuff. Attach the tufts, 2 on each side
of the head.

FEET

(make 2, in petrol blue)
Rnd 1: start 8 sc in a magic ring [8]
Rnd 2 – 3: sc in all 8 st [8]
Fasten off, leaving a long tail for sewing. Stuff
lightly with fiberfill. Sew the feet to the front,
over rounds 34 to 36.

TAIL

(in petrol blue)
Rnd 1: start 6 sc in a magic ring [6]
Rnd 2: inc in all 6 st [12]
Rnd 3: (sc in next st, inc in next st) repeat
6 times [18]
Rnd 4 – 9: sc in all 18 st [18]
Fasten off, leaving a long tail for sewing.
Use pastel pink yarn to embroider the
embellishments on the tail.

Otis Sloth

Otis had a hard time figuring out what he wanted to do in life. He's a patient guy (yes, some stereotypes hold true), but he was slowly getting bored of doing almost nothing. First, he tried to be a DJ, but Otis didn't like most of the loud, modern music. He then tried working at a restaurant, but sadly, his customers had the curious habit of wanting their food still hot. Otis decided to wait until the next opportunity presented itself (stress isn't good for your complexion), and what do you know, a new job opened up right away. His friend Lupita Spider Monkey told Otis that she needed someone to keep an eye on her space observatory at night. And that's how Otis landed his dream job, watching the night skies while lying on a comfy branch.

 GALLERY: Scan or visit www.amigurumi.com/3107 to share pictures and find inspiration.

Size:
12 inches / 30 cm tall when made with the indicated yarn

Materials:
– Worsted weight yarn in
 · mink brown
 · off-white
 · pastel pink (leftover)
 · dark warm gray (leftover)
 · yellow
 · light aqua blue (leftover)
 · greenish gray
 · black (leftover)
– Fingering or light sport weight yarn in
 · off-white
– Size B-1 / 2 mm hook
– Size C-2 / 2.75 mm hook
– Size D-3 / 3.25 mm hook
– Black safety eyes (10 mm)
– Fiberfill

Skills needed: magic ring (page 32), working around a foundation chain (page 34), changing color at the beginning of a round (page 35), changing color mid-round (page 35), working in rows, embroidery (page 38), joining parts (page 39)

Note: *Use a size C-2 / 2.75 mm crochet hook, unless otherwise noted.*

Note: *The head and body are worked in one piece.*

NOSE

(in dark warm gray)
Rnd 1: start 6 sc in a magic ring [6]
Rnd 2: inc in all 6 st [12]
Rnd 3 – 6: sc in all 12 st [12]
Rnd 7: (sc in next 3 st, inc in next st) repeat 3 times [15]
Rnd 8: sc in all 15 st [15]
Fasten off, leaving a long tail for sewing. Embroider the nose between rounds 4 and 5 over 4 stitches, with black yarn. Embroider the mouth with black yarn. Flatten the nose, it does not need to be stuffed.

CHEEKS

(make 2, in pastel pink)
Rnd 1: start 8 sc in a magic ring [8]
Slst in next st. Fasten off, leaving a long tail for sewing.

HEAD AND BODY

(start in mink brown)
Rnd 1: start 6 sc in a magic ring [6]
Rnd 2: inc in all 6 st [12]
Rnd 3: (sc in next st, inc in next st) repeat 6 times [18]
Rnd 4: (sc in next st, inc in next st) repeat 9 times [27]
Rnd 5: (sc in next 2 st, inc in next st) repeat 9 times [36]
Rnd 6: (sc in next 3 st, inc in next st) repeat 9 times [45]
Rnd 7: (sc in next 4 st, inc in next st) repeat 9 times [54]
Rnd 8: (sc in next 8 st, inc in next st) repeat 6 times [60]
Rnd 9: sc in all 60 st [60]
Continue working with alternating yarns (mink brown and off-white). The color you work with is indicated before each part.
Rnd 10: *(mink)* sc in next 21 st, *(off-white)* sc in next 18 st, *(mink)* sc in next 21 st [60]

Rnd 11: *(mink)* sc in next 20 st, *(off-white)* sc in next 20 st, *(mink)* sc in next 20 st [60]

Rnd 12: *(mink)* sc in next 18 st, *(off-white)* sc in next 4 st, *(mink)* sc in next 3 st, *(off-white)* sc in next 10 st, *(mink)* sc in next 3 st, *(off-white)* sc in next 4 st, *(mink)* sc in next 18 st [60]

Rnd 13: *(mink)* sc in next 18 st, *(off-white)* sc in next 2 st, *(mink)* sc in next 6 st, *(off-white)* sc in next 8 st, *(mink)* sc in next 6 st, *(off-white)* sc in next 2 st, *(mink)* sc in next 18 st [60]

Rnd 14 – 16: *(mink)* sc in next 26 st, *(off-white)* sc in next 8 st, *(mink)* sc in next 26 st [60]

Rnd 17: *(mink)* sc in next 20 st, *(off-white)* sc in next 2 st, *(mink)* sc in next 4 st, *(off-white)* sc in next 8 st, *(mink)* sc in next 4 st, *(off-white)* sc in next 2 st, *(mink)* sc in next 20 st [60]

Rnd 18: *(mink)* sc in next 19 st, *(off-white)* sc in next 3 st, *(mink)* sc in next 3 st, *(off-white)* sc in next 10 st, *(mink)* sc in next 3 st, *(off-white)* sc in next 3 st, *(mink)* sc in next 19 st [60]

Rnd 19: *(mink)* sc in next 20 st, *(off-white)* sc in next 20 st, *(mink)* sc in next 20 st [60]

Rnd 20: *(mink)* sc in next 22 st, *(off-white)* sc in next 16 st, *(mink)* sc in next 22 st [60]

Rnd 21: *(mink)* sc in next 24 st, *(off-white)* sc in next 12 st, *(mink)* sc in next 24 st [60]

Continue in mink brown yarn.

Rnd 22: sc in all 60 st [60]

Rnd 23: (sc in next 3 st, dec) repeat 12 times [48]

Rnd 24: (sc in next 2 st, dec) repeat 12 times [36]

Sew the nose in the middle of the white patch, between rounds 11 and 20. Insert the safety eyes between rounds 16 and 17, about 4 stitches away from the nose. Sew the cheeks to the head.

Rnd 25: (sc in next 4 st, dec) repeat 6 times [30]

Rnd 26: sc in all 30 st [30]

Stuff the head firmly. Continue in a stripe pattern, alternating 1 round in off-white and 2 rounds in greenish gray yarn.

Rnd 27: (sc in next 4 st, inc in next st) repeat 6 times [36]

Rnd 28: (sc in next 5 st, inc in next st) repeat 6 times [42]

Rnd 29 – 34: sc in all 42 st [42]

Rnd 35: (sc in next 6 st, inc in next st) repeat 6 times [48]

Rnd 36: sc in all 48 st [48]

Change to mink brown yarn.

Rnd 37: BLO sc in all 48 st [48]

Rnd 38 – 42: sc in all 48 st [48]

Rnd 43: (sc in next 6 st, dec) repeat 6 times [42]

Rnd 44: (sc in next 5 st, dec) repeat 6 times [36]

Rnd 45: (sc in next 4 st, dec) repeat 6 times [30]

Rnd 46: (sc in next 3 st, dec) repeat 6 times [24]

Rnd 47: (sc in next 2 st, dec) repeat 6 times [18]

Stuff the body firmly with fiberfill.

Rnd 48: (sc in next st, dec) repeat 6 times [12]

Rnd 49: dec 6 times [6]

Fasten off, leaving a long tail. Using a tapestry needle, weave the yarn tail through the front loop of each remaining stitch and pull tight to close. Weave in the yarn end.

LEGS

(make 2, in mink brown)
Rnd 1: start 6 sc in a magic ring [6]
Rnd 2: inc in all 6 st [12]
Rnd 3: (sc in next st, inc in next st) repeat 6 times [18]
Rnd 4: (sc in next 2 st, inc in next st) repeat 6 times [24]
Rnd 5 – 8: sc in all 24 st [24]
Rnd 9: (sc in next 6 st, dec) repeat 3 times [21]
Rnd 10 – 12: sc in all 21 st [21]
Rnd 13: (sc in next 5 st, dec) repeat 3 times [18]
Rnd 14 – 16: sc in all 18 st [18]
Rnd 17: (sc in next 4 st, dec) repeat 3 times [15]
Rnd 18 – 20: sc in all 15 st [15]
Stuff with fiberfill and continue stuffing as you go.
Rnd 21: (sc in next 3 st, dec) repeat 3 times [12]
Rnd 22 – 27: sc in all 12 st [12]
Fasten off, leaving a long tail for sewing. Add more stuffing if needed. Sew the legs on both sides between rounds 41 and 42.

ARMS

(make 2, start in mink brown)
Rnd 1: start 6 sc in a magic ring [6]
Rnd 2: inc in all 6 st [12]
Rnd 3: (sc in next st, inc in next st) repeat 6 times [18]
Rnd 4: (sc in next 5 st, inc in next st) repeat 3 times [21]
Rnd 5 – 9: sc in all 21 st [21]
Rnd 10: (sc in next 5 st, dec) repeat 3 times [18]
Rnd 11 – 14: sc in all 18 st [18]
Rnd 15: (sc in next 4 st, dec) repeat 3 times [15]
Rnd 16 – 19: sc in all 15 st [15]
Rnd 20: (sc in next 3 st, dec) repeat 3 times [12]
Rnd 21: sc in all 12 st [12]
Change to greenish gray yarn. Then continue in a

stripe pattern, alternating 1 round in off-white and 2 rounds in greenish gray yarn.
Rnd 22 – 24: sc in all 12 st [12]
Rnd 25: (sc in next 2 st, dec) repeat 3 times [9]
Fasten off, leaving a long tail for sewing. Stuff with fiberfill. Sew the arms on both sides between rounds 28 and 29.

FINGERS

(with fingering weight yarn using a size B-1 / 2 mm crochet hook, make 12, in off-white)
Rnd 1: start 6 sc in a magic ring [6]
Rnd 2 – 8: sc in all 6 st [6]
Fasten off, leaving a long tail for sewing. Do not stuff. Sew 3 fingers to each arm and 3 fingers to each leg.

HAT

(in yellow, using a size D-3/3.25 mm crochet hook)
Ch 32. Crochet in rows.
Row 1: start in third ch from the hook, hdc in next 30 st, ch 2, turn [30]
Row 2 – 27: BLO hdc in all 30 st, ch 2, turn [30]
Row 28: BLO hdc in all 30 st [30]
Fasten off, leaving a long tail for sewing. You will end with a crochet rectangle.

Using a tapestry needle and holding row 1 to row 28, sew both ends together to form a tube. Do not fasten off. With the same yarn tail, sew through the end of each row around the top of the tube. Pull the yarn tail so the round tightens, and weave in the ends by sewing back and forth to close the hat opening. Flip the hat inside out. With light aqua blue yarn, make a 2 inches / 5 cm pompon and sew it to the top of the hat.

Henriette Zebra

Henriette was born far from the city that never sleeps, but she soon found herself studying and working in art galleries in New York anyway. Henriette is happy walking the bustling and somewhat smelly streets in high heels, observing all kinds of creatures from all around the world. However, she also misses the tasty dishes she had growing up in her childhood home. A few months ago, she called her grandmother to ask her about all the recipes she knew. Since her grandmother swore she'd never set a foot in the city, Henriette challenged herself to become the best jambalaya and gumbo cook in NY. Perhaps she will end up opening a small restaurant where everyone can talk about art until the crack of dawn.

 GALLERY: Scan or visit *www.amigurumi.com/3108* to share pictures and find inspiration.

Note: Use a size C-2/2.75 mm hook for both the worsted weight yarn and the fingering weight yarn (for the top and trousers).

Size:
14 inches / 35 cm tall when made with the indicated yarn (ears included)

Materials:
– Worsted weight yarn in
 · off-white
 · graphite gray
 · light warm gray
– Fingering or light sport weight yarn in
 · pastel pink
 · brown
 · mustard (leftover)
– Size C-2 / 2.75 mm crochet hook
– Black safety eyes (oval, 12 mm)
– Fiberfill

Skills needed: magic ring *(page 32)*, working around a foundation chain *(page 34)*, changing color at the beginning of a round *(page 35)*, dividing the body in 2 parts *(page 47)*, working in rows, embroidery *(page 38)*, joining parts *(page 39)*

HEAD

(start in light warm gray)
Rnd 1: start 6 sc in a magic ring [6]
Rnd 2: inc in all 6 st [12]
Rnd 3: (sc in next st, inc in next st) repeat 6 times [18]
Rnd 4: (sc in next 2 st, inc in next st) repeat 6 times [24]
Rnd 5: (sc in next 3 st, inc in next st) repeat 6 times [30]
Rnd 6 – 11: sc in all 30 st [30]
Change to off-white yarn.
Rnd 12: sc in next 12 st, inc in next 6 st, sc in next 12 st [36]
Rnd 13: sc in all 36 st [36]
Change to graphite gray yarn.
Rnd 14: sc in next 13 st, (inc in next st, sc in next st) repeat 6 times, sc in next 11 st [42]
Continue working in a stripe pattern, alternating 5 rounds in off-white and 1 round in graphite gray yarn.
Rnd 15: sc in all 42 st [42]
Rnd 16: sc in next 14 st, (inc in next st, sc in next 2 st) repeat 6 times, sc in next 10 st [48]
Rnd 17: sc in all 48 st [48]

Rnd 18: sc in next 15 st, (inc in next st, sc in next 3 st) repeat 6 times, sc in next 9 st [54]
Rnd 19 – 29: sc in all 54 st [54]
Insert the safety eyes between rounds 22 and 23, with an interspace of 26 stitches. Embroider cheeks behind the eyes with pastel pink yarn.
Rnd 30: (sc in next 7 st, dec) repeat 6 times [48]
Rnd 31: sc in all 48 st [48]
Rnd 32: (sc in next 6 st, dec) repeat 6 times [42]
Rnd 33: (sc in next 5 st, dec) repeat 6 times [36]
Rnd 34: (sc in next 4 st, dec) repeat 6 times [30]
Rnd 35: (sc in next 3 st, dec) repeat 6 times [24]
Stuff the head firmly with fiberfill.
Rnd 36: (sc in next 2 st, dec) repeat 6 times [18]
Rnd 37: (sc in next st, dec) repeat 6 times [12]
Rnd 38: dec 6 times [6]
Fasten off, leaving a long tail. Using a tapestry needle, weave the yarn tail through the front loop of each remaining stitch and pull tight to close. Weave in the yarn end.

MANE

(in graphite gray)
Ch 23. Stitches are worked around both sides of the foundation chain.
Rnd 1: start in second ch from the hook, inc in this st, sc in next 20 st, 4 sc in next st. Continue on the other side of the foundation chain, sc in next 20 st, inc in last st [48]
Rnd 2: inc in next 2 st, sc in next 20 st, inc in next 4 st, sc in next 20 st, inc in next 2 st [56]
Rnd 3 – 6: sc in all 56 st [56]
Fasten off, leaving a long tail for sewing. Sew the mane to the back of the head and stuff as you go.

BODY

(start in off-white)
Leave a long starting yarn tail. Ch 27. Make sure your chain isn't twisted. Insert the hook in the first chain stitch and join the foundation chain with a slst. Continue working in a spiral.
Rnd 1 – 2: sc in all 27 st [27]
Change to graphite gray yarn.
Rnd 3: (sc in next 8 st, inc in next st) repeat 3 times [30]
Continue working in a stripe pattern, alternating 5 rounds in off-white and 1 round in graphite gray yarn.
Rnd 4 – 6: sc in all 30 st [30]
Rnd 7: (sc in next 4 st, inc in next st) repeat 6 times [36]
Rnd 8 – 11: sc in all 36 st [36]
Rnd 12: (sc in next 8 st, inc in next st) repeat 4 times [40]
Rnd 13 – 22: sc in all 40 st [40]

LEGS

To make the legs, divide the work identifying 4 stitches for the front central space between the legs, 4 stitches for the back and 16 stitches for each leg (you may find it useful to use stitch markers). Join the last stitch for the leg on the back side to the front side, working a single crochet stitch (this sc will be the first stitch of the leg). Now the stitches of the first leg are joined in the round. Continue working the first leg:
Rnd 23 – 26: sc in all 16 st [16]
Continue working in a stripe pattern, alternating 1 round in graphite gray and 5 rounds in off-white yarn.
Rnd 27 – 44: sc in all 16 st [16]
Change to graphite gray yarn.
Rnd 45 – 49: sc in all 16 st [16]
Stuff the body and leg firmly.
Rnd 50: (sc in next 2 st, dec) repeat 4 times [12]
Rnd 51: dec 6 times [6]
Fasten off, leaving a long tail. Using a tapestry needle, weave the yarn tail through the front loop of each remaining stitch and pull tight to close. Weave in the yarn end.

SECOND LEG
Rejoin the off-white yarn in the fifth unworked stitch at the back of round 22. Leave a long starting yarn tail. This is where we start the first stitch of the second leg.
Rnd 23: sc in all 16 st. When you reach the 16th stitch of the leg, sc in first st to join the round [16]
Rnd 24 – 51: repeat the pattern for the first leg.
Add more stuffing if needed. Using a tapestry needle, sew the 4 stitches between the legs closed. Sew the head to the body.

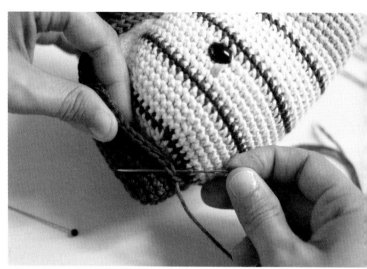

ARMS

(make 2, start in light warm gray)
Rnd 1: start 6 sc in a magic ring [6]
Rnd 2: inc in all 6 st [12]
Rnd 3 – 7: sc in all 12 st [12]
Change to off-white yarn.
Rnd 8: sc in all 12 st [12]
Change to graphite gray yarn.
Rnd 9: sc in all 12 st [12]
Continue working in a stripe pattern, alternating 5 rounds in off-white and 1 round in graphite gray yarn.
Rnd 10 – 26: sc in all 12 st [12]
Rnd 27: (sc in next st, dec) repeat 4 times [8]
Fasten off, leaving a long tail for sewing. Stuff with fiberfill. Sew the arms on both sides between rounds 3 and 4.

EARS

(make 2, start in graphite gray)
Rnd 1: start 6 sc in a magic ring [6]
Rnd 2: sc in all 6 st [6]
Rnd 3: inc in all 6 st [12]
Rnd 4: sc in all 12 st [12]
Rnd 5: (sc in next st, inc in next st) repeat 6 times [18]
Change to off-white yarn.
Rnd 6 – 13: sc in all 18 st [18]
Fasten off, leaving a long tail for sewing. Do not stuff. Flatten and pinch the ears. Sew the ears on top of the head, between rounds 27 and 30, next to the mane.

TOP

(using fingering weight yarn and a size C-2/2.75 mm crochet hook, start in brown)
Ch 37. Crochet in rows.
Row 1: start in second ch from the hook, sc in next 36 st, ch 2, turn [36]
Row 2: (hdc in next 5 st, hdc inc in next st) repeat 6 times, ch 2, turn [42]
Row 3: hdc in next 7 st, ch 6, skip next 6 st,

hdc in next 16 st, ch 6, skip next 6 st, hdc in next 7 st, ch 2, turn [42]
Row 4 – 6: hdc in all 42 st, ch 2, turn [42]
Row 7: (hdc in next 6 st, hdc inc in next st) repeat 6 times [48]
Join the last stitch of the last row to the first stitch of the next row with a half double crochet stitch (this hdc will be the first stitch of the next round). Now the stitches of the top are joined in the round. Continue working in rounds.
Rnd 8 – 10: hdc in all 48 st [48]
Change to pastel pink yarn.
Rnd 11: sc in all 48 st [48]
Fasten off and weave in the yarn ends. Insert your hook in the left side of the neckline, with the right side facing you and draw up a loop of brown yarn. Single crochet an edge all around the neckline and opening of the top, across the neck, in the row-ends down the first side and up the row-ends on the other side. Fasten off and weave in the yarn end.

TROUSERS

(using fingering weight yarn and a size C-2/2.75 mm crochet hook, in pastel pink)
Ch 46. Make sure your chain isn't twisted. Insert the hook in the first chain stitch and join the foundation chain with a slst. Continue working in a spiral.
Rnd 1 – 2: sc in all 46 st [46]

Rnd 3: (hdc in next 22 st, hdc inc in next st) repeat 2 times [48]
Rnd 4 – 5: hdc in all 48 st [48]
Rnd 6: (hdc in next 3 st, hdc inc in next st) repeat 12 times [60]
Rnd 7 – 9: hdc in all 60 st [60]

TROUSER LEGS

To make the trouser legs, divide the work identifying
5 stitches for the central space between the legs,
5 stitches for the back and 25 stitches for each trouser
leg (you may find it useful to use stitch markers). Join
the last stitch for the trouser leg on the back side to the
front side, working a half double crochet stitch (this hdc
will be the first stitch of the trouser leg). Now the stitches
of the first trouser leg are joined in the round. Continue
working the first trouser leg:
Rnd 10: hdc in all 25 st [25]
Rnd 11: (hdc in next 4 st, hdc inc in next st) repeat 5 times [30]
Rnd 12 – 13: hdc in all 30 st [30]
Rnd 14: (hdc in next 5 st, hdc inc in next st) repeat 5 times [35]
Rnd 15 – 16: hdc in all 35 st [35]
Rnd 17: (hdc in next 6 st, hdc inc in next st) repeat 5 times [40]
Rnd 18 – 19: hdc in all 40 st [40]
If the fabric bends to one side, you may want to crochet
a few more hdc before finishing with the slst round. This
way, you will be able to finish the trouser leg neatly.
Rnd 20: slst in all 40 st [40]
Fasten off and weave in the yarn ends.

SECOND TROUSER LEG

Rejoin the pastel pink yarn in the sixth unworked
stitch at the back of round 9. This is where
we start the first stitch of the second trouser leg.
Rnd 10 – 20: repeat the pattern for the first
trouser leg.
Fasten off and weave in the yarn ends.
Using a tapestry needle, sew the
5 stitches between the legs closed.

WAISTBAND
(in mustard)

Join the mustard yarn in the first stitch
of round 1 of the trousers.
Rnd 1 – 3: sc in all 46 st [46]
Fasten off and weave in the yarn ends.

Luisa Elephant

Being an elephant is not easy at all: it's almost impossible to walk into a room unnoticed and you have to be extremely careful not to trample on things. Lulú, as her loved ones call her, learned that she could only visit the houses where she fit through the door and enter a few restaurants and cafes that had enough space to fit her gorgeous body ... And let's not talk about public transportation. Luisa has a big and bright personality, but not being able to visit so many places makes her very sad. That's why Luisa now works as an urban architect and is part of a group of animals that works hard every day to change and improve life for large animals in cities around the world.

GALLERY: Scan or visit *www.amigurumi.com/3109* to share pictures and find inspiration.

Size:
12.5 inches / 31 cm tall when made with the indicated yarn

Materials:
– Worsted weight yarn in
  · light aqua blue
  · off-white
  · bright red
  · red (leftover)
  · French blue
  · ochre yellow
  · navy blue
  · pastel pink (leftover)
– Size C-2 / 2.75 mm crochet hook
– Black safety eyes (8 mm)
– Fiberfill

Skills needed: magic ring *(page 32)*, working around a foundation chain *(page 34)*, changing color at the beginning of a round *(page 35)*, dividing the body in 2 parts *(page 47)*, basket spike stitch *(page 29)*, joining parts *(page 39)*, making a pompon

Note: The head and body are worked in one piece.

Note: When crocheting the trunk, you can use the other end of your ball of yarn, so you don't need to cut your yarn or buy an extra ball.

HEAD AND BODY

(in light aqua blue)
Ch 9. Stitches are worked around both sides of the foundation chain.
Rnd 1: start in second ch from the hook, inc in this st, sc in next 6 st, 4 sc in next st. Continue on the other side of the foundation chain, sc in next 6 st, inc in last st [20]
Rnd 2: inc in next st, sc in next 8 st, inc in next 2 st, sc in next 8 st, inc in next st [24]
Rnd 3: sc in next st, inc in next st, sc in next 9 st, inc in next st, sc in next st, inc in next st, sc in next 9 st, inc in next st [28]
Rnd 4: sc in next 2 st, inc in next st, sc in next 10 st, inc in next st, sc in next 2 st, inc in next st, sc in next 10 st, inc in next st [32]
Rnd 5: sc in next 3 st, inc in next st, sc in next 11 st, inc in next st, sc in next 3 st, inc in next st, sc in next 11 st, inc in next st [36]
Rnd 6: (sc in next 5 st, inc in next st) repeat 6 times [42]

Rnd 7: (sc in next 6 st, inc in next st) repeat 6 times [48]
Rnd 8: (sc in next 7 st, inc in next st) repeat 6 times [54]
Rnd 9: (sc in next 8 st, inc in next st) repeat 6 times [60]
Note: The fabric starts to bend a lot. Do not worry, this will even out in the next few rounds.
Rnd 10 – 14: sc in all 60 st [60]
Rnd 15: sc in next 8 st, ch 12, skip next 12 st, sc in next 40 st [60]
Rnd 16 – 21: sc in all 60 st [60]
Rnd 22: (sc in next 3 st, dec) repeat 12 times [48]
Rnd 23: (sc in next 2 st, dec) repeat 12 times [36]
Rnd 24: (sc in next 4 st, dec) repeat 6 times [30]
Rnd 25: sc in all 30 st [30]
Insert the safety eyes between rounds 15 and 16, about 3 stitches away from the gap where we will be crocheting the trunk. Embroider the cheeks with pale pink yarn. Continue working the elephant trunk. Work in rounds on both sides of the trunk opening, made by the 24 st, between rounds 15 and 16.

TRUNK

Rejoin the light aqua blue yarn in the first unworked stitch at round 15. This is where we start the first stitch of the trunk.

Rnd 1 – 3: sc in all 24 st [24]
Rnd 4: sc in next 11 st, dec, sc in next 9 st, dec [22]
Rnd 5 – 7: sc in all 22 st [22]
Rnd 8: sc in next 10 st, dec, sc in next 8 st, dec [20]
Rnd 9 – 11: sc in all 20 st [20]
Rnd 12: sc in next 11 st, dec, sc in next 5 st, dec [18]
Rnd 13 – 15: sc in all 18 st [18]
Rnd 16: dec, sc in next 9 st, dec, sc in next 5 st [16]
Rnd 17 – 19: sc in all 16 st [16]
Rnd 20: dec, sc in next 8 st, dec, sc in next 4 st [14]
Rnd 21 – 23: sc in all 14 st [14]
Rnd 24: dec, sc in next 7 st, dec, sc in next 3 st [12]
Rnd 25 – 26: sc in all 12 st [12]
Rnd 27: (sc in next st, dec) repeat 4 times [8]
Fasten off, leaving a long tail for sewing. Stuff the head firmly. Stuff the trunk lightly. Sew the open end of the trunk closed. Continue working the body.

BODY

Continue working on Rnd 25 of the body.
Rnd 26: (sc in next 4 st, inc in next st) repeat 4 times, sc in next 3 st. Change to off-white yarn, sc in next st, inc in next st, sc in next 4 st, inc in next st [36]
Continue in a stripe pattern. Work 2 rounds in off-white, 1 in bright red, 2 in off-white, 1 in French blue yarn and repeat. End with one round in off-white yarn.
Rnd 27: (sc in next 5 st, inc in next st) repeat 6 times [42]
Rnd 28 – 32: sc in all 42 st [42]
Rnd 33: (sc in next 6 st, inc in next st) repeat 6 times [48]
Rnd 34 – 39: sc in all 48 st [48]
Rnd 40: (sc in next 7 st, inc in next st) repeat 6 times [54]
Rnd 41: sc in all 54 st [54]
Change to light aqua blue yarn.

Rnd 42: BLO sc in all 54 st [54]
Rnd 43 – 45: sc in all 54 st [54]
Rnd 46: (sc in next 8 st, inc in next st) repeat 6 times [60]
Rnd 47 – 51: sc in all 60 st [60]
Rnd 52: (sc in next 8 st, dec) repeat 6 times [54]
Rnd 53 – 54: sc in all 54 st [54]
Rnd 55: (sc in next 7 st, dec) repeat 6 times [48]
Rnd 56: sc in all 48 st [48]

LEGS

To make the legs, divide the work identifying 4 stitches for the front central space between the legs, 4 stitches for the back and 20 stitches for each leg (you may find it useful to use stitch markers). If the legs don't line up nicely with the head, undo a few more sc on the body. Join the last stitch for the leg on the back side to the front side, working a single crochet stitch (this sc will be the first stitch of the leg). Now the stitches of the first leg are joined in the round. Continue working the first leg:

Rnd 57 – 68: sc in all 20 st [20]
Stuff the body and leg firmly.
Rnd 69: (sc in next 2 st, dec) repeat 5 times [15]
Rnd 70: (sc in next st, dec) repeat 5 times [10]
Rnd 71: dec 5 times [5]
Fasten off, leaving a long tail. Using a tapestry needle, weave the yarn tail through the front loop of each remaining stitch and pull tight to close. Weave in the yarn end.

SECOND LEG
Rejoin the light aqua blue yarn in the fifth unworked stitch at the back of round 56. Leave a long starting yarn tail. This is where we start the first stitch of the second leg.
Rnd 57: sc in all 20 st. When you reach the 20th st of the leg, sc in first st to join the round [20]
Rnd 58 – 71: repeat the pattern for the first leg.
Add more stuffing if needed. Using a tapestry needle, sew the 4 stitches between the legs closed.

ARMS

(make 2, start in light aqua blue)
Rnd 1: start 5 sc in a magic ring [5]
Rnd 2: inc in all 5 st [10]
Rnd 3: (sc in next st, inc in next st) repeat 5 times [15]
Rnd 4 – 5: sc in all 15 st [15]
Rnd 6: sc in next st, 5-dc-bobble in next st, sc in next 13 st [15]
Rnd 7 – 18: sc in all 15 st [15]
Change to French blue yarn and continue in the same stripe pattern as used for the body.
Rnd 19 – 22: sc in all 15 st [15]
Rnd 23: (sc in next st, dec) repeat 5 times [10]
Fasten off, leaving a long tail for sewing. Stuff with fiberfill.
Sew the arms to both sides between rounds 26 and 27.

EARS

(make 2, in light aqua blue)
Rnd 1: start 6 sc in a magic ring [6]
Rnd 2: inc in all 6 st [12]
Rnd 3: sc in all 12 st [12]
Rnd 4: (sc in next st, inc in next st) repeat 6 times [18]
Rnd 5 – 6: sc in all 18 st [18]
Rnd 7: (sc in next 2 st, inc in next st) repeat 6 times [24]
Rnd 8 – 9: sc in all 24 st [24]
Rnd 10: (sc in next 3 st, inc in next st) repeat 6 times [30]
Rnd 11 – 12: sc in all 30 st [30]
Rnd 13: (sc in next 4 st, inc in next st) repeat 6 times [36]
Rnd 14 – 15: sc in all 36 st [36]
Rnd 16: (sc in next 5 st, inc in next st) repeat 6 times [42]
Rnd 17: sc in all 42 st [42]
The ear does not need to be stuffed. Next, we will divide the ear to make 3 earflaps, using 14 stitches for each flap.

FIRST FLAP
Sc in next 7 st, skip 28 st and join the last stitch to the 36th stitch of the previous round with a sc stitch.
Rnd 1 – 2: sc in all 14 st [14]
Rnd 3: (sc in next 5 st, dec) repeat 2 times [12]
Rnd 4: dec 6 times [6]

Fasten off, leaving a long tail. Using a tapestry needle, weave the yarn tail through the front loop of each remaining stitch and pull tight to close. Weave in the yarn end.

SECOND FLAP

Rejoin the light aqua blue yarn to the stitch to the left of the first flap, sc in next 7 st and join the last stitch to the seventh stitch to the right side of the first flap.

Rnd 1 – 4: repeat the pattern for the first flap.
Fasten off, leaving a long tail. Using a tapestry needle, weave the yarn tail through the front loop of each remaining stitch and pull tight to close. Weave in the yarn end.

THIRD FLAP

Rejoin the light aqua blue yarn to the stitch to the left of the second flap.

Rnd 1 – 4: repeat the pattern for the first flap.
Fasten off, leaving a long tail. Using a tapestry needle, weave the yarn tail through the front loop of each remaining stitch and pull tight to close. Weave in the yarn end.
Sew the long side of the ears to both sides of the head, between rounds 5 and 20.

TROUSERS

(in ochre yellow)
Ch 56. Make sure your chain isn't twisted. Insert the hook in the first chain stitch and join the foundation chain with a slst. Continue working in a spiral.
Rnd 1: sc in next 56 st [56]
Rnd 2: (BLO sc in next st, spike in next st of the previous round) repeat until the end of the round [56]
Rnd 3: (spike in next st of the previous round, BLO sc in next st) repeat until the end of the round [56]
Rnd 4 – 13: repeat rounds 2 and 3.

TROUSER LEGS

To make the trouser legs, divide the work identifying 4 stitches for the front central space between the legs, 4 stitches for the back and 24 stitches for each trouser leg (you may find it useful to use stitch markers). Join the last stitch for the trouser leg on the back side to the front side, working a single crochet stitch (this sc will be the first stitch of the trouser leg). Now the stitches of the first trouser leg are joined in the round. Continue working the first trouser leg:
Rnd 14: (spike in next st of the previous round, BLO sc in next st) repeat until the end of the round [24]
Rnd 15: (BLO sc in next st, spike in next st of the previous round) repeat until the end of the round [24]
Rnd 16 – 19: repeat rounds 14 and 15.
Rnd 20: slst in all 24 st [24]
Fasten off and weave in the yarn ends.

SECOND LEG
Rejoin the ochre yellow yarn in the fifth unworked stitch at the back of round 13. Leave a long starting yarn tail. This is where we start the first stitch of the second trouser leg.
Rnd 14 – 20: repeat the pattern for the first trouser leg.

Fasten off and weave in the yarn ends. Using a tapestry needle, sew the 4 stitches between the trouser legs closed.

WAISTBAND
(in ochre yellow)
Join the ochre yellow yarn in the first stitch of round 1.
Rnd 1 – 3: sc in all 56 st [56]
Rnd 4: slst in all 56 st [56]
Fasten off and weave in the yarn ends.

HAT

(in navy blue)
Rnd 1: start 8 sc in a magic ring [8]
Rnd 2: inc in all 8 st [16]
Rnd 3: (sc in next st, inc in next st) repeat 8 times [24]
Rnd 4: (sc in next 2 st, inc in next st) repeat 8 times [32]
Rnd 5: BLO sc in all 32 st [32]
Rnd 6 – 8: sc in all 32 st [32]
Slst in next st. Fasten off and weave in the yarn end.
Join the navy blue yarn in the first front loop stitch of round 5. FLO slst in all 32 st. Fasten off and weave in the yarn end.
Make a 1.5 inches / 3.5 cm pompon in red yarn and sew it to the top of the hat. Sew the hat to the head.

Anderson Seal

Anderson was born near Valdes Peninsula in Patagonia, Argentina, but now he prefers to spend most of the year in Les Eclaireurs Lighthouse, near Ushuaia (also Argentina). He sometimes longs for the warmer weather, but he definitely doesn't miss his noisy relatives gossiping and asking lots of questions. Don't get him wrong, he loves his chattering family, but he prefers to enjoy their company only once a year. Anderson spends his time collecting 35 mm films and making award-winning cheeses. He's become such a famous cheese-maker that more people are stopping by his place now. Moving the cheese production to the mainland has solved that problem, now he can continue to enjoy his quiet paradise.

 GALLERY: Scan or visit www.amigurumi.com/3110 to share pictures and find inspiration.

Size:
10.5 inches / 24 cm tall when made with the indicated yarn

Materials:
– Worsted weight yarn in
  · light aqua blue
  · pastel pink
  · off-white
  · rusty red
  · terracotta
  · greenish gray (leftover)
  · black (leftover)
– Size C-2 / 2.75 mm crochet hook
– Black safety eyes (10 mm)
– Fiberfill

Skills needed: magic ring *(page 32)*, working around a foundation chain *(page 34)*, working jacquard crochet from a diagram *(page 36)*, single rib crochet *(page 30)*, joining parts *(page 39)*, making a pompon

Note: The head and body are worked in one piece.

SNOUT

(in light aqua blue)
Rnd 1: start 6 sc in a magic ring [6]
Rnd 2: inc in all 6 st [12]
Rnd 3: (sc in next st, inc in next st) repeat 6 times [18]
Rnd 4 – 5: sc in all 18 st [18]
Fasten off, leaving a long tail for sewing. Embroider the nose and mouth with black yarn. Stuff with fiberfill. Embroider short lines on top of the nose with greenish gray yarn.

CHEEKS

(in pastel pink)
Rnd 1: start 8 sc in a magic ring [8]
Slst in next st. Fasten off, leaving a long tail for sewing.

HEAD AND BODY

(start in light aqua blue)
Rnd 1: start 6 sc in a magic ring [6]
Rnd 2: inc in all 6 st [12]
Rnd 3: (sc in next st, inc in next st) repeat 6 times [18]
Rnd 4: (sc in next 2 st, inc in next st) repeat 6 times [24]
Rnd 5: (sc in next 3 st, inc in next st) repeat 6 times [30]
Rnd 6: (sc in next 4 st, inc in next st) repeat 6 times [36]
Rnd 7: (sc in next 5 st, inc in next st) repeat 6 times [42]
Rnd 8: (sc in next 6 st, inc in next st) repeat 6 times [48]
Rnd 9: (sc in next 7 st, inc in next st) repeat 6 times [54]
Rnd 10 – 20: sc in all 54 st [54]
Sew the snout between rounds 13 and 19. The snout must be placed on the opposite side of the start of the round. Insert the safety eyes between rounds 15 and 16, about 3 stitches away from the snout. Sew the cheeks between rounds 15 and 18.

Continue in a jacquard pattern, alternating terracotta and off-white yarn (see the diagram).
Rnd 21 – 33: sc in all 54 st [54]
Change to light aqua blue yarn.
Rnd 34: BLO sc in all 54 st [54]
Rnd 35: sc in all 54 st [54]
Rnd 36: Find the middle back of the seal body. If you are not there yet, continue crocheting until that point. Then, ch 13. Place the stitch marker in the next stitch, this marks the beginning of the next round. Crochet back on the chain, start in second ch from the hook, sc in next 12 st, sc in the stitch where the foundation chain starts, continue on the body and sc in next 54 st, continue on the other side of the chain and sc in next 11 st, inc in last st [80]
Rnd 37: inc in next 2 st, sc in next 76 st, inc in next 2 st [84]
Rnd 38: inc in next 3 st, sc in next 78 st, inc in next 3 st [90]
Rnd 39 – 40: sc in all 90 st [90]
Rnd 41: sc in next 4 st, dec, sc in next st, dec, sc in next 72 st, dec, sc in next st, dec, sc in next 4 st [86]
Rnd 42: sc in next 4 st, dec, sc in next st, dec, sc in next 68 st, dec, sc in next st, dec, sc in next 4 st [82]
Rnd 43: sc in next 33 st, dec, sc in next 12 st, dec, sc in next 33 st [80]
Rnd 44: sc in next 4 st, dec, sc in next st, dec, sc in next 24 st, dec, sc in next 10 st, dec, sc in next 24 st, dec, sc in next st, dec, sc in next 4 st [74]
Rnd 45: sc in next 4 st, dec, sc in next st, dec, sc in next 22 st, dec, sc in next 8 st, dec, sc in next 22 st, dec, sc in next st, dec, sc in next 4 st [68]

Rnd 46: sc in next 4 st, dec, sc in next st, dec, sc in next 20 st, dec, sc in next 6 st, dec, sc in next 20 st, dec, sc in next st, dec, sc in next 4 st [62]
Rnd 47: sc in next 4 st, dec, sc in next 50 st, dec, sc in next 4 st [60]
Stuff the head and the first part of the body and continue stuffing as you go.
Rnd 48: (sc in next 8 st, dec) repeat 6 times [54]
Rnd 49: (sc in next 7 st, dec) repeat 6 times [48]
Rnd 50: (sc in next 6 st, dec) repeat 6 times [42]
Rnd 51: (sc in next 5 st, dec) repeat 6 times [36]
Rnd 52: (sc in next 4 st, dec) repeat 6 times [30]
Rnd 53: (sc in next 3 st, dec) repeat 6 times [24]
Rnd 54: (sc in next 2 st, dec) repeat 6 times [18]
Rnd 55: (sc in next st, dec) repeat 6 times [12]
Rnd 56: dec 6 times [6]
Fasten off, leaving a long tail. Using a tapestry needle, weave the yarn tail through the front loop of each remaining stitch and pull tight to close. Weave in the yarn end.

												33
												32
												31
												30
												29
												28
												27
												26
												25
												24
												23
												22
												21
12	11	10	9	8	7	6	5	4	3	2	1	

FLIPPERS

(make 2, in light aqua blue)
Rnd 1: start 8 sc in a magic ring [8]
Rnd 2: inc in all 8 st [16]
Rnd 3: (sc in next st, inc in next st) repeat 8 times [24]
Rnd 4: (sc in next 2 st, inc in next st) repeat 8 times [32]
Rnd 5: (sc in next 3 st, inc in next st) repeat 8 times [40]
Rnd 6: (sc in next 4 st, inc in next st) repeat 8 times [48]
Rnd 7: (sc in next 5 st, inc in next st) repeat 8 times [56]
Rnd 8: (sc in next 6 st, inc in next st) repeat 8 times [64]
Rnd 9: (sc in next 7 st, inc in next st) repeat 8 times [72]
Rnd 10: sc in all 72 st [72]
Fasten off, leaving a long tail for sewing. The flippers do not need to be stuffed. Flatten and, using a tapestry needle, close the opening of the last round. Sew the flippers on both sides between rounds 34 and 43.

TAIL

(make 2 parts, in light aqua blue)
Rnd 1: start 5 sc in a magic ring [5]
Rnd 2: inc in all 5 st [10]
Rnd 3: sc in all 10 st [10]
Rnd 4: (sc in next st, inc in next st) repeat 5 times [15]
Rnd 5 – 6: sc in all 15 st [15]
Rnd 7: (sc in next 2 st, inc in next st) repeat 5 times [20]
Rnd 8 – 9: sc in all 20 st [20]
Rnd 10: (sc in next 3 st, inc in next st) repeat 5 times [25]
Rnd 11 – 13: sc in all 25 st [25]
Fasten off, leaving a long tail for sewing. Do not stuff. Flatten and, using a tapestry needle, close the opening of the last round. Sew both parts of the tail to the body.

HAT

(in rusty red)
Rnd 1: start 6 sc in a magic ring [6]
Rnd 2: inc in all 6 st [12]
Rnd 3: (sc in next st, inc in next st) repeat
6 times [18]
Rnd 4: (sc in next 2 st, inc in next st) repeat
6 times [24]
Rnd 5: (sc in next 3 st, inc in next st) repeat
6 times [30]
Rnd 6: (sc in next 4 st, inc in next st) repeat
6 times [36]
Rnd 7: (sc in next 5 st, inc in next st) repeat
6 times [42]
Rnd 8: (sc in next 6 st, inc in next st) repeat
6 times [48]
Rnd 9: (sc in next 7 st, inc in next st) repeat
6 times [54]
Rnd 10 – 13: sc in all 54 st [54]
Rnd 14 – 16: sc rib crochet in all 54 st [54]
Fasten off and weave in the yarn ends. With
pastel pink yarn, make a 2 inches / 5 cm
pompon and sew it to the top of the hat.

James Duck

James has a little half-timbered antique shop in Rye, Sussex. Every Saturday, he wakes up early, fills his favorite red kettle (as a proper antique shop owner, James has quite a big collection of kettles and teapots, of course) and prepares himself a nice cup of tea while deciding which antique fair he's going to visit. With a thermos of delicious tea and a basket filled with cucumber sandwiches and a lovely selection of cheeses, James is a well-liked guest of any fair he visits. He always prepares special comté cheese sandwiches for his life-long friend Sebastian Lion, to enjoy when they go antique-hunting together. He usually doesn't say it out loud, but James really loves Saturdays.

 GALLERY: Scan or visit *www.amigurumi.com/3111* to share pictures and find inspiration.

Size:
11.5 inches / 29 cm tall when made with the indicated yarn

Materials:
– Worsted weight yarn in
  · teal green
  · pastel pink
  · off-white
  · petrol blue
  · yellow
  · coral
  · brown (leftover)
  · light aqua blue (leftover)
– Size C-2 / 2.75 mm crochet hook
– Black safety eyes (8 mm)
– Fiberfill

Skills needed: magic ring *(page 32)*, working around a foundation chain *(page 34)*, changing color at the beginning of a round *(page 35)*, *working* tapestry crochet *(page 36)*, dividing the body in 2 parts *(page 47)*, joining parts *(page 39)*

Note: The head and body are worked in one piece.

BEAK

(in yellow)
Ch 6. Stitches are worked around both sides of the foundation chain.
Rnd 1: start in second ch from the hook, inc in this st, sc in next 3 st, 3 sc in next st. Continue on the other side of the foundation chain, sc in next 4 st [12]
Rnd 2 – 8: sc in all 12 st [12]
Rnd 9: (sc in next 2 st, inc in next st) repeat 4 times [16]
Rnd 10: sc in all 16 st [16]
Fasten off, leaving a long tail for sewing. Stuff lightly with fiberfill.

HEAD AND BODY

(start in teal green)
Rnd 1: start 6 sc in a magic ring [6]
Rnd 2: inc in all 6 st [12]
Rnd 3: (sc in next st, inc in next st) repeat 6 times [18]
Rnd 4: (sc in next 2 st, inc in next st) repeat 6 times [24]
Rnd 5: (sc in next 3 st, inc in next st) repeat 6 times [30]
Rnd 6: (sc in next 4 st, inc in next st) repeat 6 times [36]
Rnd 7: (sc in next 5 st, inc in next st) repeat 6 times [42]
Rnd 8 – 19: sc in all 42 st [42]
Change to off-white yarn.
Rnd 20 – 21: sc in all 42 st [42]
Sew the beak between rounds 14 and 19. The beak must be placed on the opposite side of the start of the round. Insert the safety eyes between rounds 15 and 16, about 3 stitches away from the beak.
Change to pastel pink yarn.
Rnd 22 – 24: sc in all 42 st [42]

Rnd 25: sc in next 11 st, inc in next st, sc in next 19 st, inc in next st, sc in next 10 st [44]

Rnd 26 – 30: sc in all 44 st [44]

Rnd 31: (sc in next 10 st, inc in next st) repeat 4 times [48]

Rnd 32 – 38: sc in all 48 st [48]

Change to petrol blue yarn.

Rnd 39: BLO (sc in next 7 st, inc in next st) repeat 6 times [54]

Rnd 40 – 41: sc in all 54 st [54]

Rnd 42: Find the middle back of the duck body. If you are not there yet, continue crocheting until that point. Then, ch 7. Place the stitch marker in the next stitch, this marks the beginning of the next round. Crochet back on the chain, inc in second ch from the hook, sc in next 5 st, sc in the stitch where the foundation chain starts, continue on the body and sc in next 54 st, continue on the other side of the chain and sc in next 5 st, inc in last st [69]

Rnd 43: inc in next 2 st, sc in next 65 st, inc in next 2 st [73]

Rnd 44: sc in all 73 st [73]

Rnd 45: sc in next 3 st, dec, sc in next 63 st, dec, sc in next 3 st [71]

Rnd 46: sc in all 71 st [71]

Rnd 47: sc in next 3 st, dec, sc in next 23 st, dec, sc in next 12 st, dec, sc in next 22 st, dec, sc in next 3 st [67]

Rnd 48: sc in next 26 st, dec, sc in next 11 st, dec, sc in next 26 st [65]

Rnd 49: (sc in next st, dec) repeat 2 times, sc in next 20 st, dec, sc in next 9 st, dec, sc in next 21 st, dec, sc in next st, dec [59]

Rnd 50: (sc in next st, dec) repeat 2 times, sc in next 48 st, dec, sc in next st, dec [55]

Rnd 51: dec, sc in next 53 st [54]

Stuff the head and the body. Do not overstuff, so you can work the legs easily.

Rnd 52: (sc in next 7 st, dec) repeat 6 times [48]

Rnd 53: (sc in next 6 st, dec) repeat 6 times [42]

Rnd 54: (sc in next 5 st, dec) repeat 6 times [36]

LEGS

To make the legs, divide the work identifying 18 stitches for each leg. Find the middle back stitch. If you are not there yet, continue crocheting until that point or undo some stitches if needed. Ch 6 and join the last chain stitch to the 18th stitch of the previous round, working a single crochet stitch (this sc will be the first stitch of the leg). Now the stitches of the first leg are joined in the round (18 sc on the body and the ch-6 foundation chain). Continue working the first leg:

Rnd 1: sc in next 18 st on the body, BLO sc in next 6 ch [24]

Rnd 2: sc in all 24 st [24]

Rnd 3: (sc in next st, dec) repeat 8 times [16]

Change to yellow yarn.

Rnd 4: BLO (sc in next 2 st, dec) repeat 4 times [12]

Rnd 5 – 11: sc in all 12 st [12]

Fasten off, leaving a long tail for sewing. Stuff the body and the leg firmly.

SECOND LEG

Rejoin the petrol blue yarn in the first unworked stitch at the back of round 54. This is where we start the first stitch of the second leg.

Rnd 1: sc in next 18 on the body, FLO sc in next 6 ch, sc in first st to join the round [24]

Rnd 2 – 11: repeat the pattern for the first leg.

Fasten off, leaving a long tail for sewing. Stuff the leg firmly.

FOOT

(in yellow)
Rnd 1: start 6 sc in a magic ring [6]
Rnd 2: sc in all 6 st [6]
Rnd 3: inc in all 6 st [12]
Rnd 4: sc in all 12 st [12]
Rnd 5: (sc in next 3 st, inc in next st) repeat 3 times [15]
Rnd 6: sc in all 15 st [15]
Rnd 7: (sc in next 4 st, inc in next st) repeat 3 times [18]
Rnd 8: sc in all 18 st [18]
Rnd 9: (sc in next 5 st, inc in next st) repeat 3 times [21]
Rnd 10: sc in all 21 st [21]
Rnd 11: (sc in next 6 st, inc in next st) repeat 3 times [24]
Rnd 12 – 13: sc in all 24 st [24]
Fasten off, leaving a long tail for sewing. The feet do not need to be stuffed. Flatten and, using a tapestry needle, close the opening of the last round. Sew the feet to the legs.

TAIL

(make 2, start in petrol blue)
Rnd 1: start 6 sc in a magic ring [6]
Rnd 2: inc in all 6 st [12]
Rnd 3 – 10: sc in all 12 st [12]
Fasten off, leaving a long tail for sewing. The tail does not need to be stuffed. Use light aqua blue yarn to embroider the embellishments on the tail. Flatten and sew the tail to the back, centered over rounds 42 to 44.

WINGS

(make 2, start in teal green)
Start with the feathers, make 3.
Rnd 1: start 5 sc in a magic ring [5]
Rnd 2: inc in all 5 st [10]
Rnd 3 – 6: sc in all 10 st [10]
Fasten off the first and second feather. Repeat rounds 1-6 for the third feather, but do not fasten off, as we will be joining the feathers to make the wing.
Rnd 7: sc in next 4 st on the second feather, sc in all 10 st on the first feather, sc in leftover 6 st on the second feather, sc in all 10 st on the third feather [30]
You can close the holes between the feathers using your tapestry needle.
Rnd 8 – 9: sc in all 30 st [30]
Rnd 10: (sc in next 4 st, dec) repeat 5 times [25]
Rnd 11 – 12: sc in all 25 st [25]
Change to off-white yarn.
Rnd 13: sc in all 25 st [25]
Change to pastel pink yarn.
Rnd 14 – 15: sc in all 25 st [25]
Rnd 16: (sc in next 3 st, dec) repeat 5 times [20]
Rnd 17 – 19: sc in all 20 st [20]
Rnd 20: (sc in next 3 st, dec) repeat 4 times [16]
Rnd 21 – 24: sc in all 16 st [16]
Fasten off, leaving a long tail for sewing. The wings do not need to be stuffed. Flatten and sew the wings on both sides between rounds 25 and 26.

GOLF HAT

Note: *I use the tapestry crochet technique for the hat. If you are not confident using this technique, you can choose to crochet the hat in one color or in a horizontal stripe pattern.*

(start in off-white)
Rnd 1: start 8 sc in a magic ring [8]
Continue working with alternating yarns (off-white and coral). Work the second stitch in each increase in coral yarn. You will have 8 coral lines.
Rnd 2: inc in all 8 st [16]
Rnd 3: (sc in next st, inc in next st) repeat 8 times [24]
Rnd 4: (sc in next 2 st, inc in next st) repeat 8 times [32]
Rnd 5: (sc in next 3 st, inc in next st) repeat 8 times [40]
Rnd 6: (sc in next 4 st, inc in next st) repeat 8 times [48]
Rnd 7: (sc in next 5 st, inc in next st) repeat 8 times [56]
Rnd 8: (sc in next 6 st, inc in next st) repeat 8 times [64]
Rnd 9: (sc in next 7 st, inc in next st) repeat 8 times [72]
Rnd 10: (sc in next 8 st, inc in next st) repeat 8 times [80]
In the next rounds, you continue working the coral lines.
Rnd 11 – 12: ((off-white) sc in next 9 st, (coral) sc in next st) repeat 8 times [80]
Continue working each decrease in coral yarn.
Rnd 13: (sc in next 8 st, dec) repeat 8 times [72]
Rnd 14: (sc in next 7 st, dec) repeat 8 times [64]
Rnd 15: (sc in next 6 st, dec) repeat 8 times [56]
Rnd 16: (sc in next 5 st, dec) repeat 8 times [48]
Change to coral yarn.
Rnd 17 – 18: sc in all 48 st [48]
Fasten off and weave in the yarn ends. Make a 2 inch / 5 cm brown pompon and sew it to the top of the hat.

Philip Lobster

Philip was born on the coast of Picardy. Although he was born without his larger antennae, his family helped him overcome that small handicap by teaching him how to use his claws in a delicate manner. Philip achieved such great skill that the whole town called on him when they needed something done, but Philip found he liked cutting fabric the most. One day he decided it was time to share his art with the world, and with all his happiness in tow, he put on his most beloved creation, his striped shirt inspired by the coast, and got on a train to Paris. He began selling his shirts to his neighbors and acquaintances and soon, everyone was wearing his blue-striped shirts. And that's how Philip became the most famous tailor of all time, the creator of the "marinière".

GALLERY: Scan or visit www.amigurumi.com/3112 to share pictures and find inspiration.

Size:
10.5 inches / 26 cm tall when made with the indicated yarn

Materials:
– Worsted weight yarn in
 · coral
 · off-white (leftover)
 · white
 · pastel pink (leftover)
 · French blue (leftover)
 · black (leftover)
– Size C-2 / 2.75 mm crochet hook
– Black safety eyes (10 mm)
– Fiberfill

Skills needed: magic ring *(page 32)*, working around a foundation chain *(page 34)*, changing color at the beginning of a round *(page 35)*, dividing the body in 2 parts *(page 47)*, joining parts *(page 39)*

Note: The head and body are worked in one piece.

CHEEKS

(make 2, in pastel pink)
Rnd 1: start 8 sc in a magic ring [8]
Slst in next st. Fasten off, leaving a long tail for sewing.

EYE WHITES

(make 2, in off-white)
Rnd 1: start 5 sc in a magic ring [5]
Rnd 2: inc in all 5 st [10]
Slst in next st. Fasten off, leaving a long tail for sewing. Insert the safety eyes in the center of the eye whites, but do not close the washers yet.

HEAD AND BODY

(start in coral)
Start with the eyes, make 2.
Rnd 1: start 5 sc in a magic ring [5]
Rnd 2: inc in all 5 st [10]
Rnd 3: (sc in next st, inc in next st) repeat 5 times [15]
Rnd 4 – 5: sc in all 15 st [15]
Fasten off, Weave in the yarn end on the first eye. Repeat rounds 1 to 5 for the second eye, but do not fasten off as we will be joining the eyes in the next round to make the head.
Rnd 6: ch 1, sc in the last st on the first eye, sc in next 14 st on the first eye, sc in next ch, sc in next 15 st on the second eye, sc in next ch [32]
Rnd 7: (sc in next 3 st, inc in next st) repeat 8 times [40]
Rnd 8: sc in all 40 st [40]
Rnd 9: (sc in next 4 st, inc in next st) repeat 8 times [48]

Insert the safety eyes with the eye whites between rounds 4 and 5 of the eyes on the head. Close the washers and sew the eye whites to the eyes.

Rnd 10 – 13: sc in all 48 st [48]

Embroider the mouth between rounds 8 and 9 with black yarn. Sew the cheeks between rounds 8 and 11. Stuff the eyes with a bit of fiberfill.

Rnd 14 – 20: sc in all 48 st [48]

Continue in a stripe pattern, alternating 2 rounds in white and 1 round in French blue yarn.

Rnd 21 – 34: sc in all 48 st [48]

Change to coral yarn.

Rnd 35: BLO sc in next 36 st. Find the side of the body. If you're not there yet, crochet a few more sc or undo them. Ch 13. Place the stitch marker in the next st, this marks the beginning of the next round (the lobster tail). Crochet back on the chain, inc in second ch from the hook, sc in next 11 st, sc in the stitch where the foundation chain starts, continue on the body and sc in next 48 st (BLO where needed), continue on the other side of the chain and sc in next 12 st [74]

Rnd 36: inc in next 2 st, sc in next 71 st, inc in next st [77]

Rnd 37: (sc in next st, inc in next st) repeat 2 times, sc in next 72 st, inc in next st [80]

Rnd 38 – 41: sc in all 80 st [80]

Rnd 42: sc in next 4 st, dec, sc in next 70 st, dec, sc in next 2 st [78]

Rnd 43: sc in next 4 st, dec, sc in next 28 st, dec, sc in next 8 st, dec, sc in next 28 st, dec, sc in next 2 st [74]

Rnd 44: sc in next 4 st, dec, sc in next 26 st, dec, sc in next 7 st, dec, sc in next 27 st, dec, sc in next 2 st [70]

Rnd 45: sc in next 4 st, dec, sc in next 24 st, dec, sc in next 6 st, dec, sc in next 26 st, dec, sc in next 2 st [66]

Rnd 46: sc in next 4 st, dec, sc in next 22 st, dec, sc in next 5 st, dec, sc in next 25 st, dec, sc in next 2 st [62]

Rnd 47: sc in next 4 st, dec, sc in next 52 st, dec, sc in next 2 st [60]

Rnd 48: sc in all 60 st [60]

Rnd 49: (sc in next 8 st, dec) repeat 6 times [54]

Rnd 50: (sc in next 7 st, dec) repeat 6 times [48]

Stuff the head and body firmly and continue stuffing as you go.

Rnd 51: (sc in next 6 st, dec) repeat 6 times [42]

Rnd 52: (sc in next 5 st, dec) repeat 6 times [36]

Rnd 53: (sc in next 4 st, dec) repeat 6 times [30]

Rnd 54: (sc in next 3 st, dec) repeat 6 times [24]

Rnd 55: (sc in next 2 st, dec) repeat 6 times [18]

Rnd 56: (sc in next st, dec) repeat 6 times [12]

Rnd 57: dec 6 times [6]

Fasten off, leaving a long tail. Using a tapestry needle, weave the yarn tail through the front loop of each remaining stitch and pull tight to close. Weave in the yarn end.

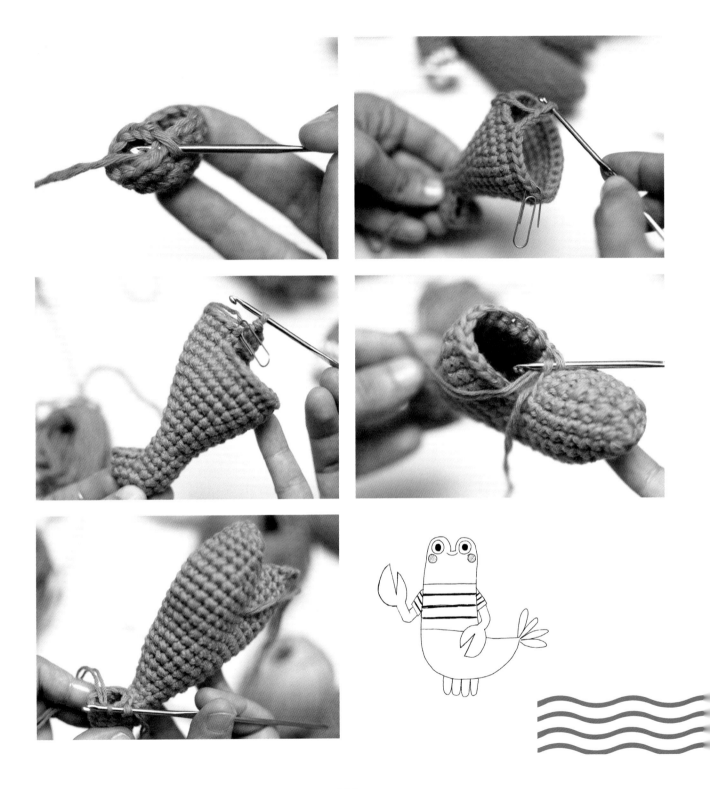

BIG CRUSHER CLAW

(in coral)

ELBOW

Rnd 1: start 6 sc in a magic ring [6]
Rnd 2: inc in all 6 st [12]
Rnd 3: (sc in next 2 st, inc in next st) repeat 4 times [16]
Rnd 4: sc in all 16 st [16]
Divide the elbow to make the 2 parts of the claw (the upper arm and the lower arm), using 8 stitches for each part.

LOWER ARM

Ch 2. Skip 8 st and join the last ch to the ninth stitch of the previous round by working a sc.
This part will be formed with 8 stitches of the elbow and the ch-2 foundation chain. Continue working the lower arm:
Rnd 1: sc in next 10 st (8 on the elbow and 2 on the chain) [10]
Rnd 2 – 3: sc in all 10 st [10]
Rnd 4: (sc in next st, inc in next st) repeat 5 times [15]
Rnd 5: sc in all 15 st [15]
Rnd 6: (sc in next 2 st, inc in next st) repeat 5 times [20]
Rnd 7: sc in all 20 st [20]
Rnd 8: (sc in next 3 st, inc in next st) repeat 5 times [25]
Rnd 9: sc in all 25 st [25]
Rnd 10: (sc in next 4 st, inc in next st) repeat 5 times [30]
Rnd 11 – 12: sc in all 30 st [30]

FIRST PART OF THE CLAW

Divide the lower arm to make the 2 parts of the claw, using 15 stitches for each part. Sc in next 7 st, ch 3, skip 15 st and join the last ch to the 16th st by working a sc.
This part will be formed with 15 stitches of the arm and the ch-3 foundation chain. Continue working the first part:
Rnd 13: sc in next 18 st (15 sc on the arm and 3 BLO sc on the chain) [18]
Rnd 14 – 15: sc in all 18 st [18]
Rnd 16: (sc in next 4 st, dec) repeat 3 times [15]
Rnd 17: sc in all 15 st [15]
Rnd 18: (sc in next 3 st, dec) repeat 3 times [12]
Rnd 19: sc in all 12 st [12]
Rnd 20: dec 6 times [6]

Fasten off, leaving a long tail. Using a tapestry needle, weave the yarn tail through the front loop of each remaining stitch and pull tight to close. Weave in the yarn end. Stuff the first part of the claw firmly.

SECOND PART OF THE CLAW

Rejoin the coral yarn to the stitch to the left of the first part of the claw.
Rnd 13: sc in next 15 st, FLO sc in next 3 ch. When you reach the 18th st of the claw, sc in first st to join the round.
Rnd 14 – 20: repeat the pattern for the first part of the claw.

UPPER ARM

Rejoin the coral yarn to the stitch to the left of the lower arm on round 4 of the elbow.
Rnd 1: sc in next 8 st, sc in next 2 ch. When you reach the 10th st of the arm, sc in first st to join the round.
Rnd 2 – 3: sc in all 10 st [10]
Continue in a stripe pattern, alternating 1 round in white and 1 round in French blue yarn.
Rnd 4 – 6: sc in all 10 st [10]
Fasten off, leaving a long tail for sewing. Stuff the arm firmly.

SMALL PINCHER CLAW

(in coral)

ELBOW

Rnd 1 – 4: repeat rounds 1 to 4 of the big crusher claw.

LOWER ARM

Ch 2. Skip 8 st and join the last ch to the ninth stitch of the previous round by working a sc.
This part will be formed with 8 stitches of the elbow and the ch-2 foundation chain. Continue working the lower arm:
Rnd 1: sc in next 10 st (8 on the elbow and 2 on the chain) [10]
Rnd 2 – 3: sc in all 10 st [10]
Rnd 4: (sc in next 4 st, inc in next st) repeat 2 times [12]

Rnd 5: (sc in next 2 st, inc in next st) repeat 4 times [16]
Rnd 6: sc in all 16 st [16]
Rnd 7: (sc in next 3 st, inc in next st) repeat 4 times [20]
Rnd 8: sc in all 20 st [20]
Rnd 9: (sc in next 4 st, inc in next st) repeat 4 times [24]
Rnd 10 – 11: sc in all 24 st [24]

FIRST PART OF THE CLAW

Divide the lower arm to make the 2 parts of the claw, using 12 stitches for each part. Sc in next 6 st, ch 3, skip 12 st and join the last ch to the 13th st by working a sc.
This part will be formed with 12 stitches of the lower arm and the ch-3 foundation chain.
Continue working the first part:
Rnd 12: sc in next 15 st (12 sc on the arm and 3 BLO sc on the chain) [15]
Rnd 13 – 14: sc in all 15 st [15]
Rnd 15: (sc in next 3 st, dec) repeat 3 times [12]
Rnd 16 – 17: sc in all 12 st [12]
Rnd 18: dec 6 times [6]
Fasten off, leaving a long tail. Using a tapestry needle, weave the yarn tail through the front loop of each remaining stitch and pull tight to close. Weave in the yarn end. Stuff the first part of the claw firmly.

SECOND PART OF THE CLAW

Rejoin the coral yarn to the stitch to the left of the first part of the claw.
Rnd 12: sc in next 12 st, FLO sc in next 3 ch. When you reach the 15th st of the claw, sc in first st to join the round.
Rnd 13 – 18: repeat the pattern for the first part of the claw.

UPPER ARM

Rnd 1 – 6: repeat rounds 1 to 6 of the big crusher claw.
Sew the arms on both sides between rounds 23 and 24.

TAIL PART

(make 4, in coral)
Rnd 1: start 5 sc in a magic ring [5]
Rnd 2: inc in all 5 st [10]
Rnd 3 – 8: sc in all 10 st [10]
Fasten off, leaving a long tail for sewing. The tail parts do not need to be stuffed. Flatten and sew them to the tail, between rounds 35 and 40.

LEGS

(make 6, in coral)
Rnd 1: start 8 sc in a magic ring [8]
Rnd 2 – 6: sc in all 8 st [8]
Fasten off, leaving a long tail for sewing. Stuff with fiberfill. Sew the six legs to the bottom of the lobster body, between rounds 51 and 55.

Lupita Spider Monkey

Since she first heard "Space Oddity", Lupita knew that she was going to devote her life to two things: go into space to travel beyond the frontiers of monkeykind and ... learn how to dance on roller skates. Lupita knows that her dreams aren't easy to achieve. She spends almost all of her time studying. And when she can no longer read another word or formula, she puts on her skates, puts on her David Bowie playlist, and goes off to practice. Studying to go to space is a challenge, but dressing in jumpsuits and sequins and dancing with roller skates without being embarrassed is one of the most difficult things anyone can think of.

 GALLERY: Scan or visit www.amigurumi.com/3113 to share pictures and find inspiration.

Size:
13.5 inches / 34 cm tall when made with the indicated yarn

Materials:
– Worsted weight yarn in
  · ochre yellow
  · off-white
  · pastel pink
  · black (leftover)
– Fingering or light sport weight yarn in
  · teal green
  · light aqua blue
  · pastel pink
– Size C-2 / 2.75 mm crochet hook
– Black safety eyes (oval, 12 mm)
– Fiberfill

Skills needed: magic ring *(page 32)*, working around a foundation chain *(page 34)*, working in rows, changing color at the beginning of a round *(page 35)*, changing color mid-round *(page 35)*, dividing the jumpsuit in 2 parts *(page 47)*, joining parts *(page 39)*

Note: The head and body are worked in one piece.

Note: Use a size C-2/2.75 mm hook for both the worsted weight yarn and the fingering weight yarn (for the jumpsuit).

SNOUT

(in off-white)
Ch 8. Stitches are worked around both sides of the foundation chain.
Rnd 1: start in second ch from the hook, sc in next 6 st, 3 sc in last st. Continue on the other side of the foundation chain, sc in next 5 st, inc in last st [16]
Rnd 2: inc in next st, sc in next 5 st, inc in next 3 st, sc in next 5 st, inc in next 2 st [22]
Rnd 3 – 5: sc in all 22 st [22]
Fasten off, leaving a long tail for sewing. Embroider the mouth and nose with black yarn. Stuff the snout lightly with fiberfill.

CHEEKS

(make 2, in pastel pink)
Rnd 1: start 6 sc in a magic ring [6]
Rnd 2: inc in all 6 st [12]
Slst in next st. Fasten off, leaving a long tail for sewing.

HEAD AND BODY

(in ochre yellow)
Rnd 1: start 6 sc in a magic ring [6]
Rnd 2: sc in all 6 st [6]
Rnd 3: (sc in next st, inc in next st) repeat 3 times [9]
Rnd 4: (sc in next 2 st, inc in next st) repeat 3 times [12]
Rnd 5: (sc in next st, inc in next st) repeat 6 times [18]
Rnd 6: (sc in next 2 st, inc in next st) repeat 6 times [24]
Rnd 7: (sc in next 3 st, inc in next st) repeat 6 times [30]
Rnd 8: (sc in next 4 st, inc in next st) repeat 6 times [36]
Rnd 9: (sc in next 5 st, inc in next st) repeat 6 times [42]
Rnd 10: (sc in next 6 st, inc in next st) repeat 6 times [48]
Rnd 11: (sc in next 7 st, inc in next st) repeat 6 times [54]
Rnd 12: (sc in next 8 st, inc in next st) repeat 6 times [60]
Continue working with alternating yarns (ochre yellow and off-white). The color you work with is indicated before each part.
Rnd 13: *(ochre yellow)* sc in next 21 st, *(off-white)* sc in next 6 st, *(ochre yellow)* sc in next 6 st, *(off-white)* sc in next 6 st, *(ochre yellow)* sc in next 21 st [60]

Rnd 14: *(ochre yellow)* sc in next 20 st, *(off-white)* sc in next 8 st, *(ochre yellow)* sc in next 4 st, *(off-white)* sc in next 8 st, *(ochre yellow)* sc in next 20 st [60]
Rnd 15: *(ochre yellow)* sc in next 19 st, *(off-white)* sc in next 10 st, *(ochre yellow)* sc in next 2 st, *(off-white)* sc in next 10 st, *(ochre yellow)* sc in next 19 st [60]
Rnd 16: *(ochre yellow)* sc in next 18 st, *(off-white)* sc in next 24 st, *(ochre yellow)* sc in next 18 st [60]
Rnd 17 – 20: *(ochre yellow)* sc in next 17 st, *(off-white)* sc in next 26 st, *(ochre yellow)* sc in next 17 st [60]
Rnd 21: *(ochre yellow)* sc in next 19 st, *(off-white)* sc in next 22 st, *(ochre yellow)* sc in next 19 st [60]
Rnd 22: *(ochre yellow)* sc in next 21 st, *(off-white)* sc in next 18 st, *(ochre yellow)* sc in next 21 st [60]
Rnd 23: *(ochre yellow)* (sc in next 3 st, dec) repeat 4 times, sc in next 3 st, *(off-white)* dec, (sc in next 3 st, dec) repeat 2 times, sc in next 2 st, *(ochre yellow)* sc in next st, dec, (sc in next 3 st, dec) repeat 4 times [48]
Continue in ochre yellow yarn.
Rnd 24: (sc in next 2 st, dec) repeat 12 times [36]
Rnd 25: (sc in next 4 st, dec) repeat 6 times [30]
Sew the snout between rounds 16 and 23, in the middle of the off-white patch. Insert the safety eyes between rounds 18 and 19, about 2 stitches away from the snout. Sew the cheeks to the head, about 3 stitches away from the snout.
Rnd 26: (sc in next st, dec) repeat 10 times [20]
Rnd 27: sc in all 20 st [20]
Stuff the head firmly with fiberfill.
Rnd 28: (sc in next st, inc in next st) repeat 10 times [30]
Rnd 29: sc in all 30 st [30]
Rnd 30: (sc in next 4 st, inc in next st) repeat 6 times [36]
Rnd 31 – 44: sc in all 36 st [36]
Rnd 45: (sc in next 4 st, dec) repeat 6 times [30]
Rnd 46: (sc in next 3 st, dec) repeat 6 times [24]
Stuff the body firmly with fiberfill.
Rnd 47: (sc in next 2 st, dec) repeat 6 times [18]
Rnd 48: (sc in next st, dec) repeat 6 times [12]
Rnd 49: dec 6 times [6]
Fasten off, leaving a long tail. Using a tapestry needle, weave the yarn tail through the front loop of each remaining stitch and pull tight to close. Weave in the yarn end.

LEGS

(make 2, start in off-white)
Rnd 1: start 6 sc in a magic ring [6]
Rnd 2: inc in all 6 st [12]
Rnd 3 – 10: sc in all 12 st [12]
Change to ochre yellow yarn.
Rnd 11 – 36: sc in all 12 st [12]
Fasten off, leaving a long tail for sewing. Stuff with fiberfill. Sew the legs to the body between rounds 43 and 44.

ARMS

(make 2, start in off-white)
Rnd 1: start 5 sc in a magic ring [5]
Rnd 2: inc in all 5 st [10]
Rnd 3 – 7: sc in all 10 st [10]
Change to ochre yellow yarn.
Rnd 8 – 26: sc in all 10 st [10]
Rnd 27: (sc in next 3 st, dec) repeat 2 times [8]
Fasten off, leaving a long tail for sewing. Stuff with fiberfill. Sew the arms on both sides between rounds 29 and 30.

EARS

(make 2, in ochre yellow)
Rnd 1: start 6 sc in a magic ring [6]
Rnd 2: inc in all 6 st [12]
Rnd 3: (sc in next st, inc in next st) repeat 6 times [18]
Rnd 4: (sc in next 2 st, inc in next st) repeat 6 times [24]
Rnd 5: sc in all 24 st [24]
Rnd 6: (sc in next 2 st, dec) repeat 6 times [18]
Rnd 7: (sc in next st, dec) repeat 6 times [12]
Rnd 8: dec 6 times [6]
Fasten off, leaving a long tail. Do not stuff. Using a tapestry needle, weave the yarn tail through the front loop of each remaining stitch and pull tight to close. Weave in the yarn end. Sew the ears between rounds 15 and 21, about 2 stitches away from the white patch of the face.

JUMPSUIT

(with 1 strand of fingering weight yarn and a size C-2/2.75 mm crochet hook, start in teal green)
Ch 34. Crochet in rows.
Row 1: start in third ch from the hook, hdc in next 32 st, ch 2, turn [32]
Continue working in a stripe pattern, alternating 1 row in teal green, 1 row in pastel pink and 1 row in light aqua blue yarn.

Row 2: (hdc in next 3 st, hdc inc in next st) repeat 8 times, ch 2, turn [40]
Row 3: hdc in next 6 st, ch 6, skip next 6 st, hdc in next 16 st, ch 6, skip next 6 st, hdc in next 6 st, ch 2, turn [40]
Work the next round in the hdc and the chain stitches.
Row 4: (hdc in next 4 st, hdc inc in next st) repeat 8 times, ch 2, turn [48]
Row 5 – 10: hdc in all 48 st, ch 2, turn [48]
Join the last stitch of the row to the first stitch of the next row, working a half double crochet stitch (this hdc

will be the first stitch of the next round). Now the stitches of the jumpsuit are joined in the round. Continue working in spirals, change to teal green yarn.

Rnd 11: (hdc in next 11 st, hdc inc in next st) repeat 4 times [52]

Rnd 12 – 13: hdc in all 52 st [52]

Rnd 14: (hdc in next 12 st, hdc inc in next st) repeat 4 times [56]

Find the middle of the jumpsuit to make the hole for the tail. If you're not there yet, work a few more sc or undo some.

Rnd 15: ch 4, skip 4 st, hdc in next 52 st [56]

Work the next round in the hdc and the chain stitches.

Rnd 16: hdc in all 56 st [56]

Rnd 17: (hdc in next 13 st, hdc inc in next st) repeat 4 times [60]

Rnd 18: hdc in all 60 st [60]

JUMPSUIT LEGS

To make the legs, divide the work identifying 6 stitches for the central space between the legs, 6 stitches for the back and 24 stitches for each leg (you may find it useful to use stitch markers). If the legs don't line up nicely with the center of the jumpsuit, crochet a few more hdc on the jumpsuit or undo them. Join the last stitch for the leg on the back side to the front side, working a half double crochet stitch (this hdc will be the first stitch of the jump-suit leg). Now the stitches of the first jumpsuit leg are joined in the round. Continue working the first jumpsuit leg:

Rnd 1 – 3: hdc in all 24 st [24]

Rnd 4: (hdc in next 11 st, hdc inc in next st) repeat 2 times [26]

Rnd 5 – 6: hdc in all 26 st [26]

Rnd 7: (hdc in next 12 st, hdc inc in next st) repeat 2 times [28]

Rnd 8 – 11: hdc in all 28 st [28]

Rnd 12: (hdc in next 13 st, hdc inc in next st) repeat 2 times [30]

Rnd 13 – 15: hdc in all 30 st [30]

If the fabric bends to one side, you may want to crochet a few more hdc before finishing with the slst round. This way you will be able to finish the jumpsuit leg neatly.

Rnd 16: slst in all 30 st [30]

Fasten off and weave in the yarn ends.

SECOND JUMPSUIT LEG

Rejoin the teal green yarn in the seventh unworked stitch at the back of round 18. Leave a long starting yarn tail. This is where we start the first stitch of the second jumpsuit leg.

Rnd 1: hdc in all 24 st. When you reach the 24th stitch of the leg, hdc in first stitch to join into the round [24]

Rnd 2 – 16: repeat the pattern for the first jumpsuit leg. Fasten off and weave in the yarn ends. Using a tapestry needle, sew the 6 stitches between the jumpsuit legs closed.

FINISHING

Insert your hook to the left of the neckline, with the right side facing you, and draw up a loop of teal green yarn. Single crochet an edge all around the top of the jumpsuit, 32 sc across the neck, about 29 sc in the row-ends down the first side, and 29 sc up the row-ends on the other side. Ch 4, slst in next st. Fasten off and weave in the yarn end.

SLEEVE RUFFLES

To make the ruffles of the sleeves, rejoin the pastel pink yarn in the last stitch before the skipped stitch of row 3. Crochet in rows. Ch 2.

Row 1: hdc inc in next 8 st, ch 2, turn [16]

Row 2: hdc inc in all 16 st [32]

Fasten off and weave in the yarn ends.

BUTTON

(with fingering weight yarn, in pastel pink)

Rnd 1: start 8 sc in a magic ring [8]

Rnd 2: sc in all 8 st [8]

Fasten off, leaving a long tail for sewing. Using a tapestry needle, weave the yarn tail through the front loop of each remaining stitch and pull tight to close. Sew the button to the back of the jumpsuit, opposite the buttonhole.

TAIL

(in ochre yellow)

Rnd 1: start 8 sc in a magic ring [8]

Stuff lightly with fiberfill as you go.

Rnd 2 – 40: sc in all 8 st [8]

Fasten off, leaving a long tail for sewing. Add more stuffing to the tail if needed. Sew the tail to the body, taking note of the position of the gap in the jumpsuit.

Monty Tamandua

Monty is a gardener who has the good fortune to live in an incredible landscape, the Valle del Lunarejo in Uruguay. He has a house at the top of "quebracho", his favorite tree, where he likes to spend most of his time, drinking mate and eating churros with honey (just a bit, because he doesn't want to abuse the generosity of his bee friends). Every day before sunset, he puts some juicy fruits and a notebook in his bag and makes his daily tour of the valley. Monty has to check the health of all the trees and make sure that the insects are doing their jobs. Monty usually prefers to be alone, but once a month he meets with René Yacaré Caiman and Marcos Coatí to exchange data on the regions they work in and discuss the book they're writing together.

Note: This toy is worked with two strands of sport weight yarn in order to create the blend of dark gray and lighter gray. Make sure to have 2 balls at hand or work with the beginning and end tail of one ball.

SKILL LEVEL ***

Size:
12.5 inches / 32 cm tall when made with the indicated yarn

Materials:
– Sport weight yarn in
· black
· light aqua blue
· off-white
· graphite gray
· pastel pink
– Size C-2 / 2.75 mm crochet hook
– Black safety eyes (8 mm)
– Fiberfill

Skills needed: working with a double strand of yarn, working between the stitches *(page 25)*, working in rows, magic ring *(page 32)*, changing color at the beginning of a round *(page 35)*, dividing the body in 2 parts *(page 47)*, joining parts *(page 39)*

HEAD

(start with 2 strands in black)
Start with the nose.
Rnd 1: start 6 sc in a magic ring [6]
Rnd 2: (sc in next st, inc in next st) repeat 3 times [9]
Rnd 3: sc in all 9 st [9]
Rnd 4: (sc in next 2 st, inc in next st) repeat 3 times [12]
Rnd 5 – 6: sc in all 12 st [12]
Rnd 7: (sc in next 3 st, inc in next st) repeat 3 times [15]
Rnd 8 – 9: sc in all 15 st [15]
Change to 1 strand in black and 1 strand in light aqua blue yarn.
Rnd 10: (sc in next 4 st, inc in next st) repeat 3 times [18]
Rnd 11 – 12: sc in all 18 st [18]
Rnd 13: (sc in next 5 st, inc in next st) repeat 3 times [21]
Rnd 14 – 15: sc in all 21 st [21]
Change to 2 strands of light aqua blue yarn.
Rnd 16: (sc in next 6 st, inc in next st) repeat 3 times [24]
Rnd 17 – 18: sc in all 24 st [24]
Rnd 19: (sc in next 7 st, inc in next st) repeat 3 times [27]
Rnd 20 – 21: sc in all 27 st [27]
Embroider short light aqua blue lines on the black part of the nose and black lines on the light aqua blue part.
Rnd 22: (sc in next 8 st, inc in next st) repeat 3 times [30]
Rnd 23 – 24: sc in all 30 st [30]

Stuff the nose and continue stuffing the head as you go.

Rnd 25: (sc in next 9 st, inc in next st) repeat 3 times [33]

Rnd 26 – 27: sc in all 33 st [33]

Rnd 28: (sc in next 10 st, inc in next st) repeat 3 times [36]

Rnd 29 – 30: sc in all 36 st [36]

Rnd 31: (sc in next 11 st, inc in next st) repeat 3 times [39]

Rnd 32 – 33: sc in all 39 st [39]

Rnd 34: (sc in next 12 st, inc in next st) repeat 3 times [42]

Rnd 35 – 37: sc in all 42 st [42]

Rnd 38: (sc in next 13 st, inc in next st) repeat 3 times [45]

Rnd 39 – 48: sc in all 45 st [45]

Insert the safety eyes between rounds 40 and 41, with an interspace of 19 stitches. Embroider little cheeks with pastel pink yarn.

Rnd 49: (sc in next 13 st, dec) repeat 3 times [42]

Rnd 50: (sc in next 5 st, dec) repeat 6 times [36]

Rnd 51: (sc in next 4 st, dec) repeat 6 times [30]

Rnd 52: (sc in next 3 st, dec) repeat 6 times [24]

Rnd 53: (sc in next 2 st, dec) repeat 6 times [18]

Rnd 54: (sc in next st, dec) repeat 6 times [12]

Rnd 55: dec 6 times [6]

Fasten off, leaving a long tail. Using a tapestry needle, weave the yarn tail through the front loop of each remaining stitch and pull tight to close. Weave in the yarn end.

BODY

(start with 2 strands in light aqua blue)

Ch 27. Make sure your chain isn't twisted. Insert the hook in the first chain stitch and join the foundation chain with a slst. Continue working in a spiral.

Rnd 1 – 2: sc in all 27 st [27]

Continue in a stripe pattern, changing color every round, alternating 2 strands of off-white and graphite gray yarn.

Rnd 3: (sc in next 8 st, inc in next st) repeat 3 times [30]

Rnd 4 – 7: sc in all 30 st [30]

Rnd 8: (sc in next 4 st, inc in next st) repeat 6 times [36]

Rnd 9 – 12: sc in all 36 st [36]

Rnd 13: (sc in next 5 st, inc in next st) repeat 6 times [42]

Rnd 14 – 17: sc in all 42 st [42]

Rnd 18: (sc in next 6 st, inc in next st) repeat 6 times [48]

Rnd 19 – 22: sc in all 48 st [48]

Change to 2 strands of light aqua blue yarn.

Rnd 23: BLO (sc in next 7 st, inc in next st) repeat 6 times [54]

Rnd 24 – 27: sc in all 54 st [54]

Rnd 28: (sc in next 8 st, inc in next st) repeat 6 times [60]

Rnd 29 – 35: sc in all 60 st [60]

Rnd 36: (sc in next 8 st, dec) repeat 6 times [54]

Rnd 37 – 40: sc in all 54 st [54]

LEGS

To make the legs, divide the work identifying 6 stitches for the front central space between the legs, 6 stitches for the back and 21 stitches for each leg (you may find it useful to use stitch markers). Join the last stitch for the leg on the back side to the front side, working a single crochet stitch (this sc will be the first stitch of the leg). Now the stitches of the first leg are joined in the round. Continue working the first leg:

Rnd 41 – 42: sc in all 21 st [21]

Change to 1 strand in black and 1 strand in light aqua blue yarn.

Rnd 43: sc in all 21 st [21]

Rnd 44: (sc in next 5 st, dec) repeat 3 times [18]

Rnd 45 – 46: sc in all 18 st [18]

Rnd 47: (sc in next 4 st, dec) repeat 3 times [15]

Change to 2 strands in black.

Rnd 48 – 49: sc in all 15 st [15]

Stuff the body and leg firmly.

Rnd 50: (sc in next 3 st, dec) repeat 3 times [12]

Rnd 51 – 52: sc in all 12 st [12]
Rnd 53: dec 6 times [6]
Fasten off, leaving a long tail. Using a tapestry needle, weave the yarn tail through the front loop of each remaining stitch and pull tight to close. Weave in the yarn end.

SECOND LEG
Rejoin the 2 strands of light aqua blue yarn to the seventh unworked stitch at the back of round 40. Leave a long starting yarn tail. This is where we start the first stitch of the second leg.
Rnd 41: sc in all 21 st. When you reach the 21st stitch of the leg, sc in first st to join the round [21]
Rnd 42 – 53: repeat the pattern for the first leg.

Add more stuffing if needed. Using a tapestry needle, sew the 6 stitches between the legs closed.
Sew the body between rounds 38 and 49 of the head.

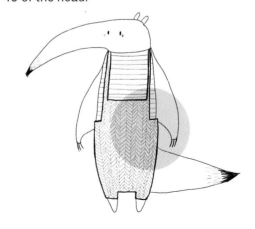

ARMS

(make 2, start with 2 strands in off-white)
Rnd 1: start 5 sc in a magic ring [5]
Rnd 2: sc in all 5 st [5]
Rnd 3: (sc in next st, inc in next st) repeat 2 times, sc in next st [7]
Rnd 4 – 5: sc in all 7 st [7]
Rnd 6: (sc in next 2 st, inc in next st) repeat 2 times, sc in next st [9]
Change to 1 strand in off-white and 1 strand in black yarn.
Rnd 7 – 8: sc in all 9 st [9]
Rnd 9: (sc in next 3 st, inc in next st) repeat 2 times, sc in next st [11]
Rnd 10 – 11: sc in all 11 st [11]
Rnd 12: (sc in next 4 st, inc in next st) repeat 2 times, sc in next st [13]
Change to 1 strand in black and 1 strand in light aqua blue yarn.
Rnd 13 – 14: sc in all 13 st [13]
Stuff lightly with fiberfill and continue stuffing as you go.
Rnd 15: (sc in next 5 st, inc in next st) repeat 2 times, sc in next st [15]
Rnd 16 – 17: sc in all 15 st [15]
Rnd 18: (sc in next 6 st, inc in next st) repeat 2 times, sc in next st [17]
Change to 2 strands of light aqua blue yarn.
Rnd 19 – 20: sc in all 17 st [17]
Rnd 21: (sc in next 7 st, inc in next st) repeat 2 times, sc in next st [19]
Rnd 22 – 30: sc in all 19 st [19]
Rnd 31: (sc in next st, dec) repeat 6 times, sc in next st [13]
Rnd 32: sc in all 13 st [13]
Fasten off, leaving a long tail for sewing. Add more stuffing to the arm if needed. Sew the arms on both sides between rounds 4 and 5.

EARS

(make 2, with 2 strands in light aqua blue)
Rnd 1: start 8 sc in a magic ring [8]
Rnd 2 – 4: sc in all 8 st [8]
Fasten off, leaving a long tail for sewing. The ears do not need to be stuffed. Flatten the ears before sewing. Sew them between rounds 47 and 48, on top of the head.

TAIL

(start with 2 strands in black)
Rnd 1: start 6 sc in a magic ring [6]
Rnd 2: sc in all 6 st [6]
Rnd 3: (sc in next st, inc in next st) repeat 3 times [9]
Rnd 4 – 5: sc in all 9 st [9]
Rnd 6: (sc in next 2 st, inc in next st) repeat 3 times [12]
Rnd 7 – 8: sc in all 12 st [12]
Rnd 9: (sc in next 3 st, inc in next st) repeat 3 times [15]
Rnd 10 – 11: sc in all 15 st [15]
Change to 1 strand in black and 1 strand in light aqua blue yarn.
Rnd 12: (sc in next 4 st, inc in next st) repeat 3 times [18]
Rnd 13 – 14: sc in all 18 st [18]
Rnd 15: (sc in next 5 st, inc in next st) repeat 3 times [21]
Rnd 16 – 17: sc in all 21 st [21]
Rnd 18: (sc in next 6 st, inc in next st) repeat 3 times [24]
Rnd 19 – 20: sc in all 24 st [24]
Rnd 21: (sc in next 7 st, inc in next st) repeat 3 times [27]
Rnd 22 – 23: sc in all 27 st [27]
Rnd 24: (sc in next 8 st, inc in next st) repeat 3 times [30]
Rnd 25 – 26: sc in all 30 st [30]
Rnd 27: (sc in next 9 st, inc in next st) repeat 3 times [33]
Rnd 28 – 29: sc in all 33 st [33]
Rnd 30: (sc in next 10 st, inc in next st) repeat 3 times [36]
Rnd 31 – 32: sc in all 36 st [36]
Rnd 33: (sc in next 11 st, inc in next st) repeat 3 times [39]
Rnd 34 – 35: sc in all 39 st [39]
Rnd 36: (sc in next 12 st, inc in next st) repeat 3 times [42]
Rnd 37 – 38: sc in all 42 st [42]
Change to 2 strands of light aqua blue yarn.
Rnd 39: (sc in next 13 st, inc in next st) repeat 3 times [45]
Rnd 40 – 42: sc in all 45 st [45]
Fasten off, leaving a long tail for sewing. Stuff with fiberfill. Sew the tail to the back, centered over rounds 23 to 37.

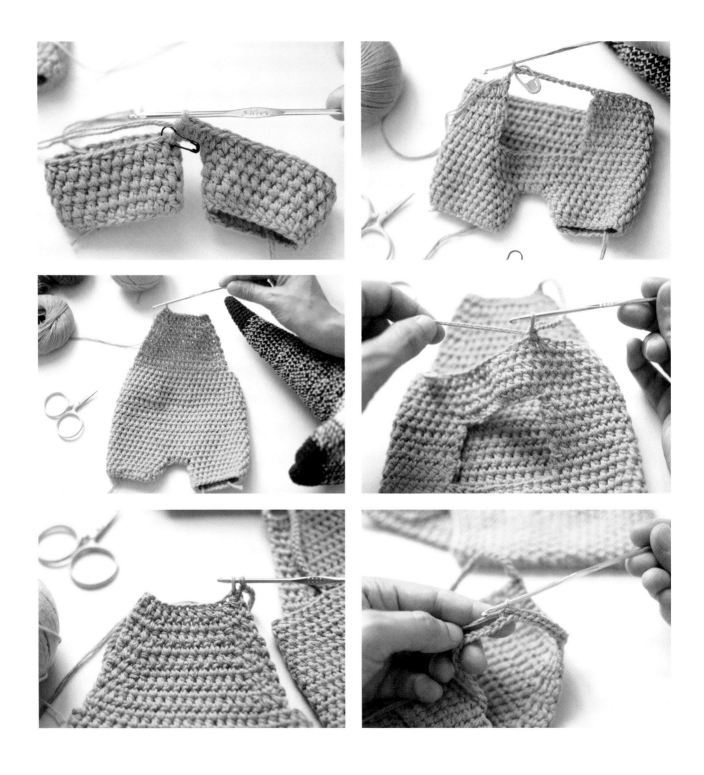

DUNGAREES

(with 2 strands in pastel pink)
Start with the dungarees legs, make 2.
Ch 24. Make sure your chain isn't twisted. Insert the hook in the first chain stitch and join the foundation chain with a slst, ch 2. Continue working in a spiral.
Rnd 1 – 4: hdc in all 24 st [24]
Fasten off and weave in the yarn end on the first leg. Repeat rounds 1 to 4 for the second leg, but do not fasten off the yarn, as we will be joining the legs in the next round to make the dungarees.
Rnd 5: ch 4, hdc into the last st on the first leg, hdc in next 23 st on the first leg, hdc in next 4 ch, hdc in next 24 st on the second leg, hdc in next 4 ch [56]
Close the hole between the legs using your tapestry needle.
Rnd 6 – 8: hdc in all 56 st [56]
Rnd 9: hdc in next 50 st. Do not finish this round. Next, create a 12 stitch space for the tail. Continue crocheting in rows. Ch 2, turn. Note that we work the stitches in Row 10-31 between the stitches, not in the top of the stitches of the previous round.
Row 10 – 14: hdc between next 44 st, ch 2, turn [44]
Row 15: hdc between next 44 st. Ch 12. Join the last ch stitch to the first st of this row, working a hdc stitch (this hdc will be the first stitch of the next round). Now the stitches of the dungarees are joined in the

round. Continue working in a spiral.
Rnd 16 – 17: hdc between next 56 st [56]
Rnd 18: (hdc between next 5 st, dec) repeat 8 times [48]
Rnd 19 – 20: hdc between next 48 st [48]
Rnd 21: hdc between next 32 st [32] Do not finish this round.
Next, crochet the front bib. Continue crocheting in rows. (Flatten the dungarees to check if you are at the outer point of the right leg. If you are not there yet, crochet a few more hdc or undo some.) Ch 2, turn.
Row 22 – 23: hdc between next 20 st, ch 2, turn [20]
Row 24: hdc between next 2 st, dec, hdc between next 12 st, dec, hdc between next 2 st, ch 2, turn [18]
Row 25: hdc between next 18 st, ch 2, turn [18]
Row 26: hdc between next 2 st, dec, hdc between next 10 st, dec, hdc between next 2 st, ch 2, turn [16]
Row 27: hdc between next 16 st, ch 2, turn [16]
Row 28: hdc between next 2 st, dec, hdc between next 8 st, dec, hdc between next 2 st, ch 2, turn [14]
Row 29: hdc between next 14 st, ch 2, turn [14]
Row 30: hdc between next 2 st, dec, hdc between next 6 st, dec, hdc between next 2 st, ch 2, turn [12]
Row 31: hdc between next 12 st [12]
Do not fasten off. Make the shoulder straps. Ch 25 and join the chain to the back of the waistband, working a sc (use the space for the tail as a reference or count 8 stitches to the left of the front bib, and join with a sc to the ninth stitch). Continue on the waistband, sc in next 11 st (you've worked 12 sc in total on the back of the waistband). Ch 25 and join the chain to the first stitch of row 31 (this sc will count as the first stitch on the front bib), sc in next 12 st on the front bib.
Rnd 32: continue on the shoulder strap chain, slst in next 25 ch, continue on the waistband, slst in next 12 st, continue on the second shoulder strap, slst in next 25 ch, continue on the top of the front bib, slst in next 12 st [74]
Fasten off and weave in the yarn end. Next, we neaten the sides of the bib. Rejoin the pastel pink yarn by inserting the hook into the outer side of the shoulder strap on the waistband. Slst in next 25 st on the shoulder strap, slst in next 13 row-ends on the left side of the front bib, slst in next 8 st on the waistband. Fasten off and weave in the yarn end. Repeat on the other side of the dungarees.

Javier Goat

Javier works along his relatives in the olive groves of his town in southern Spain. They produce the best olive oil in the region and he is super proud to be a part of this. He also has a special horticultural dream of his own: on his last trip to visit his aunt Marcia Alpaca, he fell in love with Peruvian agriculture. With the help of the seeds that Marcia gave him, Javi has begun to grow various varieties of corn, potatoes and tomatoes on his land. His dream is to cultivate all the variety that once existed in South America, recover the original flavors and treat the earth gently. While waiting for his crops to grow, he spends hours knitting, and he is thinking about learning how to dye and spin his own yarn as well.

 GALLERY: Scan or visit *www.amigurumi.com/3115* to share pictures and find inspiration.

 ***

Size:
13 inches / 33 cm tall when made with the indicated yarn (horns included)

Materials:
– Worsted weight yarn in
  · brown
  · off-white
  · graphite gray
  · yellow
  · black (leftover)
  · pastel pink (leftover)
– Size C-2 / 2.75 mm crochet hook
– Black safety eyes (10 mm)
– Fiberfill

Skills needed: magic ring *(page 32)*, working around a foundation chain *(page 34)*, changing color at the beginning of a round *(page 35)*, changing color mid-round *(page 35)*, working in rows, dividing the body in 2 parts *(page 47)*, moss stitch *(page 28)*, embroidery *(page 38)*, joining parts *(page 39)*

Note: The head and body are worked in one piece.

CHEEKS

(make 2, in pastel pink)
Rnd 1: start 8 sc in a magic ring [8]
Slst in next st. Fasten off, leaving a long tail for sewing.

SNOUT

(in off-white)
Rnd 1: start 6 sc in a magic ring [6]
Rnd 2: inc in all 6 st [12]
Rnd 3: (sc in next st, inc in next st) repeat 6 times [18]
Rnd 4: (sc in next 2 st, inc in next st) repeat 6 times [24]
Rnd 5 – 7: sc in all 24 st [24]
Rnd 8: (sc in next 5 st, inc in next st) repeat 4 times [28]
Rnd 9: sc in all 28 st [28]
Fasten off, leaving a long tail for sewing. Embroider the nose and the mouth with black yarn. Stuff the snout with fiberfill.

HEAD AND BODY

(start in brown)
Rnd 1: start 6 sc in a magic ring [6]
Rnd 2: inc in all 6 st [12]
Rnd 3: (sc in next st, inc in next st) repeat 6 times [18]
Continue working with alternating yarns (brown and off-white). The color you work with is indicated before each part.
Rnd 4: *(brown)* (sc in next 2 st, inc in next st) repeat 2 times, *(off-white)* sc in next 2 st, inc in next st, sc in next 2 st, *(brown)* inc in next st, (sc in next 2 st, inc in next st) repeat 2 times [24]
Rnd 5: *(brown)* (sc in next 3 st, inc in next st) repeat 2 times, *(off-white)* sc in next 3 st, inc in next st, sc in next 2 st, *(brown)* sc in next st, inc in next st, (sc in next 3 st, inc in next st) repeat 2 times [30]
Rnd 6: *(brown)* (sc in next 4 st, inc in next st) repeat 2 times, *(off-white)* sc in next 4 st, inc in next st, sc in next 2 st, *(brown)* sc in next 2 st, inc in next st, (sc in next 4 st, inc in next st) repeat 2 times [36]
Rnd 7: *(brown)* (sc in next 5 st, inc in next st) repeat 2 times, *(off-white)* sc in next 5 st, inc in next st, sc in next 2 st,

(brown) sc in next 3 st, inc in next st, (sc in next 5 st, inc in next st) repeat 2 times [42]

Rnd 8: (brown) (sc in next 6 st, inc in next st) repeat 2 times, (off-white) sc in next 6 st, inc in next st, sc in next 2 st, (brown) sc in next 4 st, inc in next st, (sc in next 6 st, inc in next st) repeat 2 times [48]

Rnd 9: (brown) (sc in next 7 st, inc in next st) repeat 2 times, (off-white) sc in next 7 st, inc in next st, sc in next 2 st, (brown) sc in next 5 st, inc in next st, (sc in next 7 st, inc in next st) repeat 2 times [54]

Rnd 10: (brown) (sc in next 8 st, inc in next st) repeat 2 times, (off-white) sc in next 8 st, inc in next st, sc in next 2 st, (brown) sc in next 6 st, inc in next st, (sc in next 8 st, inc in next st) repeat 2 times [60]

Rnd 11 – 15: (brown) sc in next 20 st, (off-white) sc in next 12 st, (brown) sc in next 28 st [60]

Rnd 16: (brown) sc in next 21 st, (off-white) sc in next 10 st, (brown) sc in next 29 st [60]

Rnd 17 – 18: (brown) sc in next 22 st, (off-white) sc in next 8 st, (brown) sc in next 30 st [60]

Continue in brown yarn.

Rnd 19 – 23: sc in all 60 st [60]

Continue working with alternating yarns (brown and off-white). The color you work with is indicated before each line.

Rnd 24: (brown) (sc in next 3 st, dec) repeat 4 times, sc in next st, (off-white) sc in next 2 st, dec, sc in next 3 st, dec, sc in next 2 st, (brown) sc in next st, dec, (sc in next 3 st, dec) repeat 5 times [48]

Rnd 25: (brown) (sc in next 2 st, dec) repeat 4 times, sc in next st, (off-white) sc in next st, dec, sc in next 2 st, dec, sc in next 2 st, (brown) dec, (sc in next 2 st, dec) repeat 5 times [36]

Sew the snout between rounds 17 and 25. Insert the safety eyes between rounds 18 and 19, about 3 stitches away from the snout. Sew the cheeks below the eyes.

Rnd 26: (brown) (sc in next 4 st, dec) repeat 2 times, sc in next st, (off-white) sc in next 3 st, dec, sc in next 2 st, (brown) sc in next 2 st, dec, (sc in next 4 st, dec) repeat 2 times [30]

Rnd 27: (brown) (sc in next 3 st, dec) repeat 2 times, sc in next st, (off-white) sc in next 2 st, dec, sc in next 2 st, (brown) sc in next st, dec, (sc in next 3 st, dec) repeat 2 times [24]

Rnd 28: (brown) sc in next 4 st, dec, sc in next 3 st, (off-white) sc in next st, dec, sc in next 2 st, (brown) sc in next 2 st, dec, sc in next 4 st, dec [20]

Rnd 29: (brown) sc in next 8 st, (off-white) sc in next 4 st, (brown) sc in next 8 st [20]

Stuff the head firmly. Continue in a stripe pattern, changing color every round, alternating graphite gray and off-white yarn.

Rnd 30: (sc in next st, inc in next st) repeat 10 times [30]

Rnd 31 – 32: sc in all 30 st [30]

Rnd 33: (sc in next 4 st, inc in next st) repeat 6 times [36]

Rnd 34 – 37: sc in all 36 st [36]

Rnd 38: (sc in next 8 st, inc in next st) repeat 4 times [40]

Rnd 39 – 41: sc in all 40 st [40]

Change to brown yarn.

Rnd 42: BLO sc in all 40 st [40]

Rnd 43 – 47: sc in all 40 st [40]

LEGS

To make the legs, divide the work identifying 4 stitches for the front central space between the legs, 4 stitches for the back and 16 stitches for each leg (you may find it useful to use stitch markers). If the legs don't line up nicely with the head, crochet a few more sc on the body or undo them. Join the last stitch for the leg on the back side to the front side, working a single crochet stitch (this sc will be the first stitch of the leg). Now the stitches of the first leg are joined in the round. Continue working the first leg:

Rnd 48 – 73: sc in all 16 st [16]
Stuff the body and leg firmly.
Rnd 74: (sc in next 2 st, dec) repeat 4 times [12]
Rnd 75: dec 6 times [6]
Fasten off, leaving a long tail. Using a tapestry needle, weave the yarn tail through the front loop of each remaining stitch and pull tight to close. Weave in the yarn end.

SECOND LEG
Rejoin the brown yarn in the fifth unworked stitch at the back of round 47. This is where we start the first stitch of the second leg. Leave a long starting yarn tail.
Rnd 48: sc in all 16 st. When you reach the 16th st of the leg, sc in first stitch to join the round [16]
Rnd 49 – 75: repeat the pattern for the first leg.
Stuff the second leg and add more stuffing to the body if needed. Using a tapestry needle, sew the 4 stitches between the legs closed.

ARMS

(make 2, start in brown)
Rnd 1: start 6 sc in a magic ring [6]
Rnd 2: inc in all 6 st [12]
Rnd 3 – 4: sc in all 12 st [12]
Rnd 5: sc in next st, 5-dc-bobble in next st, sc in next 10 st [12]
Rnd 6 – 17: sc in all 12 st [12]
Continue in a stripe pattern, changing color every round, alternating graphite gray and off-white yarn.

Rnd 18 – 20: sc in all 12 st [12]
Rnd 21: (sc in next st, dec) repeat 4 times [8]
Fasten off, leaving a long tail for sewing. Stuff with fiberfill. Sew the arms to both sides between rounds 31 and 32.

HORNS

(make 2, in off-white)
Rnd 1: start 6 sc in a magic ring [6]
Rnd 2: sc in all 6 st [6]
Rnd 3: BLO (sc in next st, inc in next st) repeat 3 times [9]
Rnd 4: sc in all 9 st [9]
Rnd 5: BLO (sc in next 2 st, inc in next st) repeat 3 times [12]
Rnd 6: sc in all 12 st [12]
Rnd 7: BLO sc in all 12 st [12]
Rnd 8: sc in all 12 st [12]
Fasten off, leaving a long tail for sewing. Stuff lightly with fiberfill. Sew the horns on top of the head, over rounds 4 to 8.

EARS

(make 2, in brown)
Rnd 1: start 6 sc in a magic ring [6]
Rnd 2: inc in all 6 st [12]
Rnd 3: sc in all 12 st [12]
Rnd 4: (sc in next st, inc in next st) repeat 6 times [18]
Rnd 5 – 6: sc in all 18 st [18]
Rnd 7: (sc in next 2 st, inc in next st) repeat 6 times [24]
Rnd 8 – 14: sc in all 24 st [24]
Rnd 15: (sc in next 4 st, dec) repeat 4 times [20]
Rnd 16 – 17: sc in all 20 st [20]
Rnd 18: (sc in next 3 st, dec) repeat 4 times [16]
Rnd 19 – 20: sc in all 16 st [16]
Fasten off, leaving a long tail for sewing. Do not stuff. Embroider off-white stripes on the inside of the ear. Flatten and pinch the ears. Sew the ears on top of the head, over rounds 9 to 11.

BEARD

(in off-white)
Rnd 1: start 5 sc in a magic ring [5]
Rnd 2: sc in all 5 st [5]
Rnd 3: (sc in next st, inc in next st) repeat 2 times, sc in next st [7]
Rnd 4: sc in all 7 st [7]
Fasten off, leaving a long tail for sewing. Stuff lightly. Sew the beard to the bottom of the snout, over rounds 7 to 9.

TAIL

(in brown)
Rnd 1: start 5 sc in a magic ring [5]
Rnd 2: sc in all 5 st [5]
Rnd 3: inc in all 5 st [10]
Rnd 4: sc in all 10 st [10]
Fasten off, leaving a long tail for sewing. Do not stuff. Sew the tail to the back, centered over rounds 42 and 43.

DUNGAREES

(start in graphite gray)
Ch 48. Make sure your chain isn't twisted. Insert the hook in the first chain stitch and join the foundation chain with a slst. Continue working in a spiral.
Rnd 1: sc in all 48 st [48]
Rnd 2: (sc in next 23 st, inc in next st) repeat 2 times [50]
Continue working in a jacquard pattern, alternating rounds with 2 st in graphite gray and 1 st in off-white yarn, with plain graphite gray rounds (see the diagram).
Rnd 3: sc in all 50 st [50]
Rnd 4: sc in next 2 st, ch 5, skip next 5 st, sc in next 43 st [50]
Rnd 5 – 9: sc in all 50 st [50]

DUNGAREES LEGS

To make the dungarees legs, divide the work identifying 4 stitches for the central space between the legs, 4 stitches for the back and 21 stitches for each dungarees leg. Make sure the hole for the tail is in the middle. Join the last stitch for the dungarees leg on the back side to the front side, working a single crochet stitch (this sc will be the first stitch of the next round). Now the stitches of the first dungarees leg are joined in the round. Continue working the first dungarees leg.

Rnd 10 – 20: (in a jacquard pattern) sc in all 21 st [21]
Rnd 21: (in graphite gray) slst in all 21 st [21]
Fasten off and weave in the yarn ends.

SECOND LEG
Rejoin the graphite gray yarn in the fifth unworked stitch at the back of round 10. This is where we start the first stitch of the second dungarees leg.
Rnd 10 – 21: repeat the pattern for the first dungarees leg.
Fasten off and weave in the yarn ends. Using a tapestry needle, sew the 4 stitches between the legs closed.

DUNGAREES FRONT BIB

(in yellow)
Continue working the front bib. Crochet in rows on the center 12 stitches of round 1. Insert your hook with the right side facing you and draw up a loop.
Row 1: sc in all 12 st, ch 1, turn [12]
Row 2 – 7: moss stitch in all 12 st, ch 1, turn [12]
Row 8: moss stitch in all 12 st [12]
Do not fasten off. Make the shoulder straps and waistband. Ch 21, start in second ch from the hook, slst in next 20 ch. Continue on the top of the front bib, slst in next 12 st, ch 21, start in second ch from the hook, slst in next 20 ch, sc in next 8 row-ends. Continue on the waistband, sc in next 7 st, dec, sc in next 19 st, dec, sc in next 7 st. Continue on the right side of the front bib, sc in next 8 row-ends.
Fasten off and weave in the yarn ends. Cross the shoulder straps at the back and sew them to the dungarees.

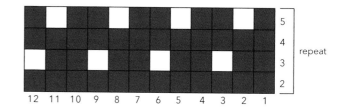

Nira Tigress

Nira has always described herself as a crafter. Weaving, crocheting, knitting, macramé, you name it, she has mastered all of these techniques. She also has a second job: she's a designer at a technology lab where she applies all her crafts to create fabrics of sustainable and recycled materials that can be used in different areas of science and construction. But Nira doesn't usually talk about her job a lot, because many people get bored with the technicalities, or simply think she's bragging about it. She prefers to go unnoticed, sitting quietly in a cafe, knitting scarves while imagining how to tackle the next big fabric challenge.

 GALLERY: Scan or visit *www.amigurumi.com/3116* to share pictures and find inspiration.

Size:
12.5 inches / 32 cm tall when made with the indicated yarn (ears included)

Materials:
– Worsted weight yarn in
· pastel pink
· off-white
· black (leftover)
· rusty red
· yellow
· greenish gray
– Fingering (crocheted double) or light worsted weight yarn in
· teal green
– Size C-2 / 2.75 mm crochet hook
– Size D-3 / 3.25 mm crochet hook
– Black safety eyes (10 mm)
– Fiberfill

Skills needed: magic ring *(page 32)*, working around a foundation chain *(page 34)*, changing color at the beginning of a round *(page 35)*, changing color mid-round *(page 35)*, dividing the body in 2 parts *(page 47)*, basket spike stitch *(page 29)*, embroidery *(page 38)*, joining parts *(page 39)*

Note: *Use a size C-2 / 2.75 mm crochet hook, unless otherwise noted.*

Note: *The head and body are worked in one piece.*

Note: *This design was made using X-shaped sc (page 23). If you are using V-shaped stitches, the stripes will be aligned on one side and widen at the other side. You may have to move the stripes so they are positioned in the middle.*

SNOUT

(start in off-white)
Ch 8. Stitches are worked around both sides of the foundation chain.
Rnd 1: start in second ch from the hook, inc in this st, sc in next 5 st, 3 sc in next st. Continue on the other side of the foundation chain, sc in next 6 st [16]
Continue working with alternating yarns (off-white and pastel pink). The color you work with is indicated before each part.
Rnd 2: *(off-white)* inc in next 2 st, sc in next 5 st, inc in next 2 st, *(pastel pink)* inc in next st, sc in next 5 st, inc in next st [22]
Rnd 3 – 5: *(pastel pink)* sc in next st, *(off-white)* sc in next 12 st, *(pastel pink)* sc in next 9 st [22]
Fasten off, leaving a long tail for sewing. Embroider the nose and mouth with black yarn. Stuff the snout with fiberfill.

HEAD AND BODY

(start in pastel pink)
Rnd 1: start 6 sc in a magic ring [6]
Rnd 2: inc in all 6 st [12]
Rnd 3: (sc in next st, inc in next st) repeat 6 times [18]
Rnd 4: (sc in next 2 st, inc in next st) repeat 6 times [24]
Rnd 5: (sc in next 3 st, inc in next st) repeat 6 times [30]
Rnd 6: (sc in next 4 st, inc in next st) repeat 6 times [36]
Continue working with alternating yarns (pastel pink and rusty red). The color you work with is indicated before each part.
Rnd 7: *(pastel pink)* (sc in next 5 st, inc in next st) repeat 3 times, *(rusty red)* sc in next 5 st, *(pastel pink)* inc in next st, (sc in next 5 st, inc in next st) repeat 2 times [42]

Rnd 8: *(pastel pink)* (sc in next 6 st, inc in next st) repeat 6 times [48]

Rnd 9: *(pastel pink)* (sc in next 7 st, inc in next st) repeat 6 times [54]

Rnd 10: *(pastel pink)* sc in next 26 st, *(rusty red)* sc in next 8 st, *(pastel pink)* sc in next 20 st [54]

Rnd 11 – 12: *(pastel pink)* sc in all 54 st [54]

Rnd 13: *(pastel pink)* sc in next 25 st, *(rusty red)* sc in next 10 st, *(pastel pink)* sc in next 19 st [54]

Rnd 14: *(pastel pink)* sc in all 54 st [54]

Rnd 15: *(pastel pink)* (sc in next 8 st, inc in next st) repeat 6 times [60]

Rnd 16: *(pastel pink)* sc in next 13 st, *(rusty red)* sc in next 10 st, *(pastel pink)* sc in next 20 st, *(rusty red)* sc in next 10 st, *(pastel pink)* sc in next 7 st [60]

Rnd 17: *(pastel pink)* sc in all 60 st [60]

Change to off-white yarn.

Rnd 18: (sc in next 4 st, inc in next st) repeat 12 times [72]

Rnd 19 – 22: sc in all 72 st [72]

Rnd 23: (sc in next 4 st, dec) repeat 12 times [60]

Rnd 24: (sc in next 3 st, dec) repeat 12 times [48]

Rnd 25: (sc in next 2 st, dec) repeat 12 times [36]

Sew the snout between rounds 15 and 22, below the 3 rusty red lines. Insert the safety eyes between rounds 16 and 17, about 2 stitches away from the snout.

Rnd 26: (sc in next 4 st, dec) repeat 6 times [30]

Rnd 27: (sc in next 3 st, dec) repeat 6 times [24]

Rnd 28: (sc in next 4 st, dec) repeat 4 times [20]

Rnd 29: sc in all 20 st [20]

Change to greenish gray yarn.

Rnd 30: (sc in next 4 st, inc in next st) repeat 4 times [24]

Rnd 31: (sc in next 3 st, inc in next st) repeat 6 times [30]

Rnd 32 – 33: sc in all 30 st [30]

Rnd 34: (sc in next 4 st, inc in next st) repeat 6 times [36]

Rnd 35 – 36: sc in all 36 st [36]

Rnd 37: (sc in next 8 st, inc in next st) repeat 4 times [40]

Rnd 38 – 40: sc in all 40 st [40]

Change to pastel pink yarn.

Rnd 41: BLO sc in all 40 st [40]

Rnd 42: sc in all 40 st [40]

In the next rounds, work rusty red lines on both sides of the body. These should be aligned with the lines on the side of the head. If they don't match, crochet a few more sc or undo some.

Rnd 43: *(pastel pink)* sc in next 10 st, *(rusty red)* sc in next 10 st, *(pastel pink)* sc in next 10 st, *(rusty red)* sc in next 10 st [40]

Rnd 44 – 45: *(pastel pink)* sc in next 40 st [40]

Rnd 46: *(pastel pink)* sc in next 10 st, *(rusty red)* sc in next 10 st, *(pastel pink)* sc in next 10 st, *(rusty red)* sc in next 10 st [40]

LEGS

To make the legs, divide the work identifying 4 stitches for the front central space between the legs, 4 stitches for the back and 16 stitches for each leg (you may find it useful to use stitch markers). If the legs don't line up nicely with the head, crochet a few more sc on the body or undo them. Join the last stitch for the leg on the back side to the front side, working a single crochet stitch (this sc will be the first stitch of the leg). Now the stitches of the first leg are joined in the round. Continue working the first leg:

Rnd 47 – 48: *(pastel pink)* sc in all 16 st [16]

In the next round we work the last rusty red line. This line should be aligned with the lines higher up on the body. If they don't match, crochet a few more sc or undo some.

Rnd 49: *(pastel pink)* sc in next 2 st, *(rusty red)* sc in next 10 st, *(pastel pink)* sc in next 4 st [16]

Continue working in pastel pink yarn.

Rnd 50 – 72: sc in all 16 st [16]

Stuff the body and leg firmly with fiberfill.

Rnd 73: (sc in next 2 st, dec) repeat 4 times [12]

Rnd 74: dec 6 times [6]

Fasten off, leaving a long tail. Using a tapestry needle, weave the yarn tail through the front loop of each remaining stitch and pull tight to close. Weave in the yarn end.

SECOND LEG

Rejoin the pastel pink yarn in the fifth unworked stitch at the back of round 46. Leave a long starting yarn tail. This is where we start the first stitch of the second leg.

Rnd 47: sc in all 16 st. When you reach the 16th st of the leg, sc in first st to join the round [16]

Rnd 48 – 74: repeat the pattern for the first leg. Add more stuffing to the body if needed. Using a tapestry needle, sew the 4 stitches between the legs closed.

ARMS

(make 2, start in pastel pink)
Rnd 1: start 6 sc in a magic ring [6]
Rnd 2: inc in all 6 st [12]
Rnd 3 – 4: sc in all 12 st [12]
Rnd 5: sc in next st, 5-dc-bobble in next st, sc in next 10 st [12]
Rnd 6 – 17: sc in all 12 st [12]
Change to greenish gray yarn.
Rnd 18 – 20: sc in all 12 st [12]
Rnd 21: (sc in next st, dec) repeat 4 times [8]
Fasten off, leaving a long tail for sewing. Stuff with fiberfill. Sew the arms on both sides between rounds 31 and 32.

EARS

(make 2, start in black)
Rnd 1: start 6 sc in a magic ring [6]
Rnd 2: inc in all 6 st [12]
Continue working with alternating yarns (pastel pink and off-white). The color you work with is indicated before each part.
Rnd 3: *(pastel pink)* (sc in next st, inc in next st) repeat 4 times, *(off-white)* (sc in next st, inc in next st) repeat 2 times [18]
Rnd 4 – 7: *(pastel pink)* sc in next 12 st, *(off-white)* sc in next 6 st [18]
Fasten off, leaving a long tail for sewing. Do not stuff. Flatten the ears. Sew them to the head.

SKIRT

(in teal green)
Ch 40. Make sure your chain isn't twisted. Insert the hook in the first chain stitch and join the foundation chain with a slst. Continue working in a spiral.
Rnd 1: hdc in all 40 st [40]
Rnd 2: (hdc in next 4 st, hdc inc in next st) repeat 8 times [48]
Rnd 3: (hdc in next 5 st, hdc inc in next st) repeat 8 times [56]
Rnd 4: (hdc in next 6 st, hdc inc in next st) repeat 8 times [64]
Rnd 5: (hdc in next 7 st, hdc inc in next st) repeat 8 times [72]
Rnd 6: (hdc in next 8 st, hdc inc in next st) repeat 8 times [80]
Rnd 7: (hdc in next 9 st, hdc inc in next st) repeat 8 times [88]
Rnd 8: (hdc in next 10 st, hdc inc in next st) repeat 8 times [96]
Rnd 9: (hdc in next 11 st, hdc inc in next st) repeat 8 times [104]
Rnd 10: (hdc in next 12 st, hdc inc in next st) repeat 8 times [11
Rnd 11: hdc in all 112 st [112]
Rnd 12: slst in all 112 st [112]
Fasten off and weave in the yarn ends.

WAISTBAND
(in teal green)
Join the teal green yarn in the first stitch of round 1 of the skirt.
Rnd 1 – 3: sc in all 40 st [40]
Fasten off and weave in the yarn ends.

TAIL

(start in rusty red)
Rnd 1: start 5 sc in a magic ring [5]
Rnd 2: inc in all 5 st [10]
Rnd 3 – 5: sc in all 10 st [10]
Change to pastel pink yarn. Continue in a stripe pattern, alternating 3 rounds in pastel pink and 2 rounds in rusty red yarn. Stuff lightly with fiberfill and continue stuffing as you go.
Rnd 6 – 43: sc in all 10 st [10]
Fasten off, leaving a long tail for sewing. Add more stuffing to the tail if needed. Sew the tail to the back, centered over round 43.

COWL

(using a size D-3 / 3.25 mm hook, start in yellow)
Ch 50. Make sure your chain isn't twisted. Insert the hook in the first chain stitch and join the foundation chain with a slst. Continue working in a spiral.
Rnd 1: sc in all 50 st [50]
Rnd 2: (BLO sc in next st, spike in the st of the previous round) repeat until the end of the round. Change to off-white yarn.
Rnd 3: (spike in the st of the previous round, BLO sc in next st) repeat until the end of the round. Change to yellow yarn.
Rnd 4: (BLO sc in next st, spike in the st of the previous round) repeat until the end of the round.
Rnd 5: (spike in the st of the previous round, BLO sc in next st) repeat until the end of the round. Change to off-white yarn.
Rnd 6 – 11: repeat rounds 3 to 5 two more times. Fasten off and weave in the yarn ends.

Sebastian Lion

As a screenwriter and a puppeteer, Bastian knew exactly what he wanted to be from the first minute of the first time he watched "The Dark Crystal". He couldn't believe his own eyes, all the work behind the scenes, the months (even years) needed to create such a fantastic animated world using only dolls and strings (and a lot of pretty intricate mechanics, but that's something he would learn later). That same day he began to build his first puppet. Luckily, his friend James Duck (who had just started collecting antiques) got Bastian all the necessary materials to set up the sceneries and props. Over time, he gathered a small puppet company and after having worked on several major animated films and series, he's now working hard on his writing skills to venture into the world as a screenwriter.

GALLERY: Scan or visit *www.amigurumi.com/3117* to share pictures and find inspiration.

SKILL LEVEL ∗∗∗

Size:
11 inches / 28 cm tall when made with the indicated yarn

Materials:
– Worsted weight yarn in
  · ochre yellow
  · brown (Note: the mane requires the same amount of yarn as the body.)
  · off-white
  · white
  · petrol blue
  · pastel pink
  · black (leftover)
– Size C-2 / 2.75 mm crochet hook
– Black safety eyes (8 mm)
– Fiberfill

Skills needed: magic ring *(page 32)*, changing color at the beginning of a round *(page 35)*, working in rows, dividing the body in 2 parts *(page 47)*, embroidery *(page 38)*, joining parts *(page 39)*

SNOUT

(start in black)
Rnd 1: start 6 sc in a magic ring [6]
Rnd 2: inc in all 6 st [12]
Rnd 3: sc in all 12 st [12]
Change to ochre yellow yarn.
Rnd 4: (sc in next 3 st, inc in next st) repeat 3 times [15]
Rnd 5 – 21: sc in all 15 st [15]
Fasten off, leaving a long tail for sewing. The snout does not need to be stuffed. Flatten the snout. Embroider short brown lines on top of it.

HEAD AND BODY

(start in off-white)
Rnd 1: start 6 sc in a magic ring [6]
Rnd 2: inc in all 6 st [12]
Rnd 3: (sc in next st, inc in next st) repeat 6 times [18]
Rnd 4: (sc in next 2 st, inc in next st) repeat 6 times [24]
Rnd 5: (sc in next 3 st, inc in next st) repeat 6 times [30]
Rnd 6: sc in all 30 st [30]
Change to ochre yellow yarn.
Rnd 7 – 8: sc in all 30 st [30]
Rnd 9: sc in next 14 st, inc in next 2 st, sc in next 14 st [32]
Rnd 10 – 11: sc in all 32 st [32]
Rnd 12: (sc in next 7 st, inc in next st) repeat 4 times [36]

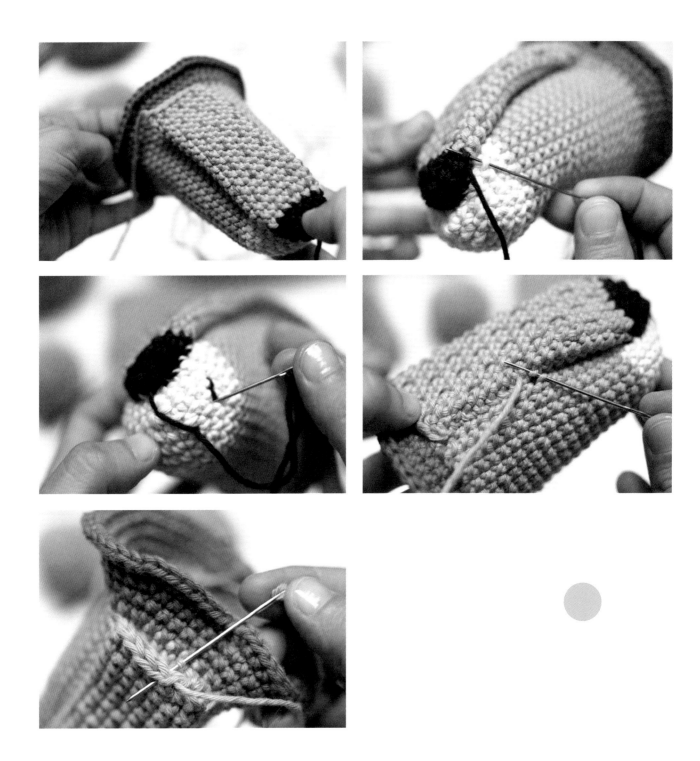

Rnd 13 – 15: sc in all 36 st [36]
Rnd 16: (sc in next 8 st, inc in next st) repeat 4 times [40]
Rnd 17 – 19: sc in all 40 st [40]
Rnd 20: (sc in next 9 st, inc in next st) repeat 4 times [44]
Rnd 21 – 22: sc in all 44 st [44]
Change to brown yarn. Next, make the base for the lion's mane.
Note: *In the pattern we work the brown part in both loops. You may choose to work in BLO if this makes assembly of the mane easier for you.*
Rnd 23: sc in next 7 st, inc in next st, (sc in next 5 st, inc in next st) repeat 5 times, sc in next 6 st [50]
Rnd 24: sc in all 50 st [50]
Rnd 25: sc in next 8 st, inc in next st, (sc in next 6 st, inc in next st) repeat 5 times, sc in next 6 st [56]
Rnd 26: sc in next 9 st, inc in next st, (sc in next 7 st, inc in next st) repeat 5 times, sc in next 6 st [62]
Sew the snout to the head between rounds 2 and 22. The snout must be placed on the opposite side of the start of the round. Take the increases from the mane into account to center the nose. Embroider the mouth with black yarn. Insert the safety eyes between rounds 19 and 20, about 3 stitches away from the nose. Using pastel pink yarn, embroider a small cheek behind the eye.
Rnd 27: sc in next 19 st, inc in next st, (sc in next 8 st, inc in next st) repeat 3 times, sc in next 15 st [66]
Rnd 28 – 30: sc in all 66 st [66]
Rnd 31: (sc in next 9 st, dec) repeat 6 times [60]
Rnd 32: (sc in next 8 st, dec) repeat 6 times [54]
Rnd 33: (sc in next 7 st, dec) repeat 6 times [48]
Rnd 34: (sc in next 6 st, dec) repeat 6 times [42]
Rnd 35: (sc in next 5 st, dec) repeat 6 times [36]
Rnd 36: (sc in next 4 st, dec) repeat 6 times [30]
Stuff the head firmly with fiberfill.
Rnd 37: (sc in next 3 st, dec) repeat 6 times [24]
Rnd 38: (sc in next 2 st, dec) repeat 6 times [18]
Rnd 39: (sc in next st, dec) repeat 6 times [12]

Rnd 40: dec 6 times [6]
Fasten off, leaving a long tail. Using a tapestry needle, weave the yarn tail through the front loop of each remaining stitch and pull tight to close. Weave in the yarn end.

BODY

(start in ochre yellow)
Leave a long starting yarn tail. Ch 24. Make sure your chain isn't twisted. Insert the hook in the first chain stitch and join the foundation chain with a slst. Continue working in a spiral.
Rnd 1 – 2: sc in all 24 st [24]
Change to petrol blue yarn.
Rnd 3: (sc in next 3 st, inc in next st) repeat 6 times [30]
Rnd 4 – 6: sc in all 30 st [30]
Rnd 7: (sc in next 4 st, inc in next st) repeat 6 times [36]
Rnd 8 – 10: sc in all 36 st [36]
Rnd 11: (sc in next 8 st, inc in next st) repeat 4 times [40]
Rnd 12 – 13: sc in all 40 st [40]
Change to ochre yellow yarn.
Rnd 14: BLO sc in all 40 st [40]
Rnd 15 – 20: sc in all 40 st [40]

LEGS

To make the legs, divide the work identifying 2 stitches for the front central space between the legs, 2 stitches for the back and 18 stitches for each leg (you may find it useful to use stitch markers). Join the last stitch for the leg on the back side to the front side, working a single crochet stitch (this sc will be the first stitch of the leg). Now the stitches of the first leg are joined in the round. Continue working the first leg:
Rnd 21 – 46: sc in all 18 st [18]
Stuff the body and leg firmly.
Rnd 47: (sc in next st, dec) repeat 6 times [12]
Rnd 48: dec 6 times [6]
Fasten off, leaving a long tail. Using a tapestry needle, weave the yarn tail through the front loop of each remaining stitch and pull tight to close. Weave in the yarn end.

SECOND LEG

Rejoin the ochre yellow yarn in the third unworked stitch at the back of round 20. Leave a long starting yarn tail. This is where we start the first stitch of the second leg.

Rnd 21: sc in all 18 st. When you reach the 18th stitch of the leg, sc in first st to join the round [18]

Rnd 22 – 48: repeat the pattern for the first leg.

Add more stuffing if needed. Using a tapestry needle, sew the 2 stitches between the legs closed. Sew the head to the body. The head must be attached firmly because it has to support quite a lot of hair.

EARS

(make 2, in ochre yellow)
Rnd 1: start 6 sc in a magic ring [6]
Rnd 2: inc in all 6 st [12]
Rnd 3 – 5: sc in all 12 st [12]
Fasten off, leaving a long tail for sewing. Do not stuff. Flatten the ears and sew them to rounds 25 and 26 of the head.

MANE

(in brown)
Insert the hook on the side of the first brown round of the head.
Ch 8. Join with a slst in the next st on the head. Continue working the hair in all stitches of the first round of the mane. Repeat this for all brown rounds, now working ch 10 loops. When you reach the neck area, work ch 12 loops.

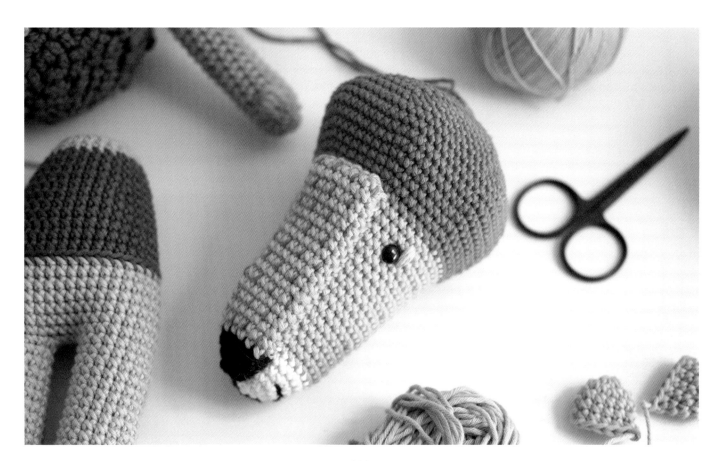

ARMS

(make 2, start in ochre yellow)
Rnd 1: start 6 sc in a magic ring [6]
Rnd 2: inc in all 6 st [12]
Rnd 3 – 4: sc in all 12 st [12]
Rnd 5: sc in next st, 5-dc-bobble in next st, sc in next 10 st [12]
Rnd 6 – 18: sc in all 12 st [12]
Change to petrol blue yarn.
Rnd 19 – 21: sc in all 12 st [12]
Rnd 22: (sc in next st, dec) repeat 4 times [8]
Fasten off, leaving a long tail for sewing. Stuff with fiberfill. Sew the arms on both sides between rounds 3 and 4.

TAIL

(in ochre yellow)
Rnd 1: start 8 sc in a magic ring [8]
Remember to stuff lightly with fiberfill and continue stuffing as you go.
Rnd 2 – 40: sc in all 8 st [8]
Fasten off, leaving a long tail for sewing. Add more stuffing to the tail if needed. Sew the tail to the back, centered over round 15.

SHORTS

(start in petrol blue)
Ch 44. Make sure your chain isn't twisted. Insert the hook in the first chain stitch and join the foundation chain with a slst. Continue working in a spiral.
Work in a stripe pattern, changing color every round, alternating petrol blue and white yarn.
Rnd 1 – 4: sc in all 44 st [44]
Rnd 5: sc in next 37 st, ch 5, skip next 5 st, sc in next 2 st [44]
Rnd 6: sc in all 44 st [44]
Rnd 7: (sc in next 10 st, inc in next st) repeat 4 times [48]
Rnd 8 – 10: sc in all 48 st [48]
Rnd 11: (sc in next 11 st, inc in next st) repeat 4 times [52]
Rnd 12 – 13: sc in all 52 st [52]

SHORTS LEGS

To make the shorts legs, divide the work identifying 2 stitches for the central space between the legs, 2 stitches for the back and 24 stitches for each shorts leg (you may find it useful to use stitch markers). Make sure the hole for the tail in round 5 is centered on the bottom. Join the last stitch for the shorts leg on the back side to the front side, working a single crochet stitch (this sc will be the first stitch of the shorts leg). Now the stitches of the first short leg are joined in the round. Continue working the first shorts leg in a stripe pattern:
Rnd 14 – 20: sc in all 24 st [24]
Rnd 21: slst in all 24 st [24]
Fasten off and weave in the yarn ends.

SECOND SHORTS LEG

Rejoin the white yarn in the third un-worked stitch at the back of round 13. This is where we start the first stitch of the second shorts leg.

Rnd 14 – 21: repeat the pattern for the first short leg.

Fasten off and weave in the yarn ends. Using a tapestry needle, sew the 2 stitches between the legs closed.

WAISTBAND
(start in white)

Join the white yarn in the first stitch of round 1.

Rnd 1: sc in all 44 st [44]

Change to pastel pink yarn.

Rnd 2: sc in all 44 st [44]

Rnd 3: slst in all 44 st [44]

Fasten off and weave in the yarn ends.

SCARF

(in pastel pink)

Ch 110. Crochet in rows.

Row 1: start in third ch from the hook, hdc in all 108 st, ch 2, turn [108]

Row 2 – 3: BLO hdc in all 108 st, ch 2, turn [108]

Row 4: BLO hdc in all 108 st [108]

Fasten off and weave in the yarn ends.

Thomas Aguará Guazú

Thomas was born somewhere between Argentina, Paraguay and Brazil. He doesn't know exactly where and the truth is that he couldn't care less about it. Thomas strongly believes that borders are ridiculous and we should have stopped using that concept a long time ago, but he does research the borders and the life in those regions. He takes his job very seriously, but that doesn't mean that he is not a fun guy. Thomas loves a good party and doesn't miss a chance to wear his superb bow tie, a gift from his friend Daniel Jack Russell. He's also set to travel to the Galápagos Islands, where he'll will meet up with Newton Owl and Darwin Turtle to start filming a documentary about the deep interrelation of all things in this world.

GALLERY: Scan or visit *www.amigurumi.com/3118* to share pictures and find inspiration.

SKILL LEVEL *

Size:
11 inches / 28 cm tall when made with the indicated yarn (standing, ears included)

Materials:
– Worsted weight yarn in
  · terracotta
  · off-white
  · black
  · pastel pink (leftover)
  · light aqua blue
  · graphite gray
– Size C-2 / 2.75 mm crochet hook
– Black safety eyes (10 mm)
– Fiberfill

Skills needed: magic ring *(page 32)*, working around a foundation chain *(page 34)*, working in rows, changing color at the beginning of a round *(page 35)*, working jacquard from a diagram *(page 36)*, dividing the body in 4 parts, embroidery *(page 38)*, joining parts *(page 39)*

Note: The head and body are worked in one piece.

CHEEKS

(make 2, in pastel pink)
Rnd 1: start 6 sc in a magic ring [6]
Slst in next st. Fasten off, leaving a long tail for sewing.

SNOUT

(start in black)
Rnd 1: start 6 sc in a magic ring [6]
Rnd 2: inc in all 6 st [12]
Rnd 3 – 6: sc in all 12 st [12]
Change to off-white yarn.
Rnd 7: (sc in next st, inc in next st) repeat 6 times [18]
Rnd 8 – 9: sc in all 18 st [18]
Continue working with alternating yarns (off-white and terracotta). The color you work with is indicated before each part.
Rnd 10: *(off-white)* sc in next 6 st, *(terracotta)* sc in next 2 st, inc in next 2 st, sc in next 2 st, *(off-white)* sc in next 6 st [20]
Rnd 11: *(off-white)* sc in next 6 st, *(terracotta)* sc in next 8 st, *(off-white)* sc in next 6 st [20]
Rnd 12: *(off-white)* sc in next 6 st, *(terracotta)* sc in next 2 st, inc in next 4 st, sc in next 2 st, *(off-white)* sc in next 6 st [24]
Rnd 13: *(off-white)* sc in next 6 st, *(terracotta)* sc in next 12 st, *(off-white)* sc in next 6 st [24]
Fasten off, leaving a long tail for sewing.
Embroider the mouth with black yarn.
Stuff the snout with fiberfill.

HEAD AND BODY

(start in terracotta)
Rnd 1: start 6 sc in a magic ring [6]
Rnd 2: inc in all 6 st [12]
Rnd 3: (sc in next st, inc in next st) repeat 6 times [18]
Rnd 4: (sc in next 2 st, inc in next st) repeat 6 times [24]
Rnd 5: (sc in next 3 st, inc in next st) repeat 6 times [30]
Rnd 6: (sc in next 4 st, inc in next st) repeat 6 times [36]
Rnd 7: (sc in next 5 st, inc in next st) repeat 6 times [42]
Rnd 8: (sc in next 6 st, inc in next st) repeat 6 times [48]
Rnd 9: (sc in next 7 st, inc in next st) repeat 6 times [54]

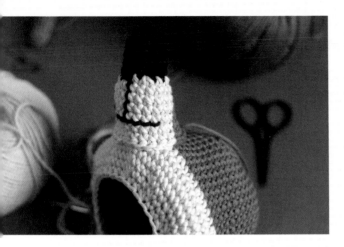

Rnd 32: inc in next 2 st, sc in next 24 st, inc in next st, sc in next st, inc in next st, sc in next 24 st, inc in next st [59]
Rnd 33: (sc in next st, inc in next st) repeat 2 times, sc in next 54 st, inc in next st [62]
Rnd 34: (sc in next 2 st, inc in next st) repeat 2 times, sc in next 55 st, inc in next st [65]
Rnd 35: sc in next 2 st, inc in next st, sc in next 3 st, inc in next st, sc in next 26 st, inc in next st, sc in next 2 st, inc in next st, sc in next 26 st, inc in next st, sc in next st [70]
Rnd 36 – 45: sc in all 70 st [70]

LEGS

We have to divide the work to crochet the four legs.

FIRST BACK LEG
First, find the middle back stitch of the body. If you are not there yet, continue crocheting until that point.
Then, sc in next 2 st. Place a stitch marker in the next stitch.
Sc in next 11 st, ch 7. Join the last ch and the stitch with the stitch marker by working a slst.
The leg will be formed with 11 sc of the body and the ch-7 foundation chain. Continue working the first back leg:
Rnd 1: sc in next 18 st (11 on the body and 7 on the chain) [18]
Rnd 2 – 6: sc in all 18 st [18]
Change to black yarn.
Rnd 7: BLO (sc in next 4 st, dec) repeat 3 times [15]
Rnd 8 – 10: sc in all 15 st [15]
Rnd 11: (sc in next 3 st, dec) repeat 3 times [12]
Rnd 12 – 15: sc in all 12 st [12]
Rnd 16: dec 6 times [6]
Fasten off, leaving a long tail. Using a tapestry needle, weave the yarn tail through the front loop of each remaining stitch and pull tight to close. Weave in the yarn end.

Rnd 10: (sc in next 8 st, inc in next st) repeat 6 times [60]
Rnd 11 – 18: sc in all 60 st [60]
Change to off-white yarn.
Rnd 19: (sc in next 3 st, inc in next st) repeat 15 times [75]
Rnd 20 – 22: sc in all 75 st [75]
Rnd 23: (sc in next 3 st, dec) repeat 15 times [60]
Rnd 24: (sc in next 3 st, dec) repeat 12 times [48]
Rnd 25: (sc in next 2 st, dec) repeat 12 times [36]
Sew the snout between rounds 15 and 22. The snout must be placed on the opposite side of the start of the round. Insert the safety eyes between rounds 17 and 18, about 3 stitches away from the snout. Sew the cheeks behind the eyes.
Rnd 26: (sc in next 4 st, dec) repeat 6 times [30]
Rnd 27: (sc in next 3 st, dec) repeat 6 times [24]
Rnd 28: (sc in next 4 st, dec) repeat 4 times [20]
Stuff the head. Change to terracotta yarn.
Rnd 29: sc in all 20 st [20]
Rnd 30: (sc in next 4 st, inc in next st) repeat 4 times [24]
Rnd 31: Find the opposite side of the snout. If you're not there yet, crochet a few more sc on the head or undo them. Ch 15. Place the stitch marker in the next st, this marks the beginning of the next round. Crochet back on the chain, inc in second ch from the hook, sc in next 13 ch, sc in the st where the foundation chain starts, continue on the neck and sc in next 24 st, continue on the other side of the chain and sc in next 14 st [54]

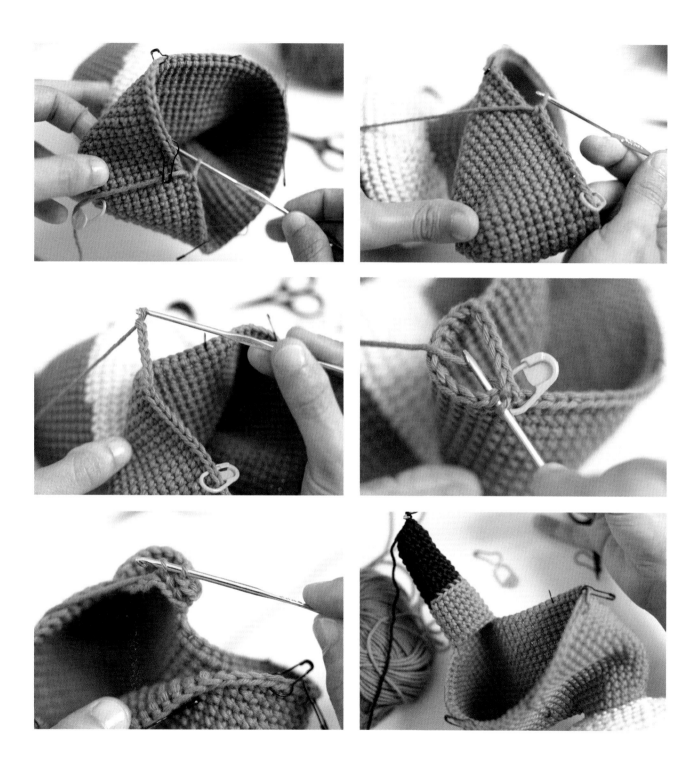

FIRST FRONT LEG

Count 9 stitches along from the first back leg (this will become the belly) and attach terracotta yarn to the 10th stitch.

Sc in next 11 st, ch 7 and join the last ch and the first sc stitch with a slst.

Rnd 1 – 16: repeat rounds 1-16 of the first back leg.

SECOND FRONT LEG

Count 4 st to the left of the first front leg (this is the space between the legs) and attach terracotta yarn to the 5th stitch.

Sc in next 11 st, ch 7 and join the last ch and the first sc stitch with a slst.

Rnd 1 – 16: repeat rounds 1-16 of the first back leg.

SECOND BACK LEG

Count 9 st to the left of the second front leg (this is the other side of the belly) and attach terracotta yarn to the 10th stitch.

Sc in next 11 st, ch 7 and join the last ch and the first sc stitch with a slst.

Rnd 1 – 16: repeat rounds 1-16 of the first back leg.

BELLY

Between the legs you have 9 stitch spaces along the sides and 4 stitch spaces at the front and back. Make the belly by crocheting flaps on these stitches. Start with the 9 stitch spaces along the side. Attach terracotta yarn to the first stitch next to the first leg you made. Crochet in rows.

Row 1 – 12: sc in next 9 st, ch 1, turn [9]

Fasten off, leaving a long tail for sewing.

FLAP BETWEEN THE LEGS

For the back flap, attach terracotta yarn to the first stitch next to the last leg you made. Crochet in rows.

Row 1 – 4: sc in next 4 st, ch 1, turn [4]

Fasten off, leaving a long tail for sewing. Work the flap between the front legs in the same way.

ASSEMBLY OF THE BODY

Using a tapestry needle, sew the front flap to both front legs and the back flap to both back legs.
Stuff each leg firmly with fiberfill.
Sew the wide belly flap to the other side of the body.
Then sew the belly flap to both legs and the flaps between them, stuffing the body as you go.

EARS

(make 2, start in black)
Rnd 1: start 6 sc in a magic ring [6]
Rnd 2: sc in all 6 st [6]
Rnd 3: (sc in next st, inc in next st) repeat 3 times [9]
Rnd 4: sc in all 9 st [9]
Rnd 5: (sc in next 2 st, inc in next st) repeat 3 times [12]
Change to terracotta yarn.
Rnd 6: sc in all 12 st [12]
Rnd 7: (sc in next 3 st, inc in next st) repeat 3 times [15]
Rnd 8: sc in all 15 st [15]
Rnd 9: (sc in next 4 st, inc in next st) repeat 3 times [18]
Rnd 10: sc in all 18 st [18]
Rnd 11: (sc in next 5 st, inc in next st) repeat
3 times [21]
Rnd 12 – 15: sc in all 21 st [21]
Fasten off, leaving a long tail for sewing. The ears do not need to be stuffed. Embroider off-white stripes on the inside of the ears. Flatten the ears before sewing them on the head.

TAIL

(start in off-white)
Rnd 1: start 6 sc in a magic ring [6]
Rnd 2: inc in all 6 st [12]
Rnd 3: (sc in next st, inc in next st) repeat 6 times [18]
Rnd 4: (sc in next 2 st, inc in next st) repeat 6 times [24]
Rnd 5: sc in all 24 st [24]
Rnd 6: (sc in next 3 st, inc in next st) repeat 6 times [30]
Rnd 7: sc in all 30 st [30]
Rnd 8: (sc in next 4 st, inc in next st) repeat 6 times [36]
Rnd 9 – 11: sc in all 36 st [36]
Change to terracotta yarn.
Rnd 12 – 16: sc in all 36 st [36]
Rnd 17: (sc in next 7 st, dec) repeat 4 times [32]
Rnd 18 – 19: sc in all 32 st [32]
Rnd 20: (sc in next 6 st, dec) repeat 4 times [28]
Rnd 21 – 22: sc in all 28 st [28]

Rnd 23: (sc in next 5 st, dec) repeat 4 times [24]
Rnd 24 – 25: sc in all 24 st [24]
Rnd 26: (sc in next 4 st, dec) repeat 4 times [20]
Rnd 27 – 28: sc in all 20 st [20]
Rnd 29: (sc in next 3 st, dec) repeat 4 times [16]
Rnd 30 – 31: sc in all 16 st [16]
Rnd 32: (sc in next 2 st, dec) repeat 4 times [12]
Rnd 33 – 34: sc in all 12 st [12]
Fasten off, leaving a long tail for sewing. Stuff with fiberfill. Sew the tail to the back, centered over rounds 32 and 33.

BOW TIE

(start in graphite gray)
Ch 40. Make sure your chain isn't twisted. Insert the hook in the first chain stitch and join the foundation chain with a slst. Continue working in a spiral in a jacquard pattern, alternating graphite gray and light aqua blue yarn (see the diagram).
Rnd 1 – 13: sc in all 40 st [40]
Fasten off and weave in the yarn end.

MIDDLE RIBBON
(in graphite gray)
Ch 17. Do not join.
Row 1: start in second ch from the hook, sc in next 16 ch [16]
Fasten off, leaving a long tail for sewing. Pinch the bow tie together and sew the middle ribbon around the center of the bow tie. Sew the bow tie to the neck.

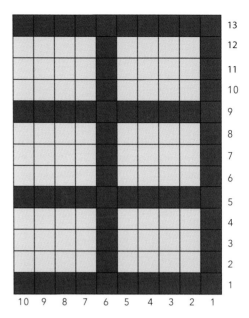

Ada Lamb

Ada was raised by her Italian grandmother, an opera lover. Although at first she didn't quite understand how anyone could be a fan of such loud singing, Ada fell in love with music and the opera herself when her grandmother showed her the cartoons she used to watch in her childhood, the "Silly Symphonies". And well, the rest is history ... Ada has not only become the youngest lamb orchestra conductor, but she's also an astonishingly talented soprano who has taken concert halls around the world by storm with her incredible energy and passion. At least once a year she visits Italy to enjoy her favorite activity in the whole world, to sit and watch cartoons with her grandmother while drinking an aperitif.

GALLERY: Scan or visit *www.amigurumi.com/3119* to share pictures and find inspiration.

Size:
8 inches / 20 cm tall when made with the indicated yarn (standing, ears included)

Materials:
– Worsted weight yarn in
  · off-white
  · pastel pink
  · black (leftover)
– Fingering weight yarn in
  · off-white
  · pastel pink
  · green
– Size C-2 / 2.75 mm crochet hook
– Size D-3 /3.25 mm crochet hook
– Black safety eyes (10 mm)
– Fiberfill

Skills needed: magic ring *(page 32)*, working around a foundation chain *(page 34)*, changing color at the beginning of a round *(page 35)*, working in rows, working tapestry crochet *(page 36)*, dividing the body in 4 parts *(page 158)*, embroidery *(page 38)*, joining parts *(page 39)*

HEAD

(in off-white)
Rnd 1: start 6 sc in a magic ring [6]
Rnd 2: inc in all 6 st [12]
Rnd 3: (sc in next st, inc in next st) repeat 6 times [18]
Rnd 4: (sc in next 2 st, inc in next st) repeat 6 times [24]
Rnd 5: sc in all 24 st [24]
Rnd 6: (sc in next 5 st, inc in next st) repeat 4 times [28]
Rnd 7: sc in all 28 st [28]
Rnd 8: (sc in next 6 st, inc in next st) repeat 4 times [32]
Rnd 9: sc in all 32 st [32]
Rnd 10: (sc in next 7 st, inc in next st) repeat 4 times [36]
Rnd 11: sc in all 36 st [36]
Rnd 12: (sc in next 8 st, inc in next st) repeat 4 times [40]
Rnd 13: sc in all 40 st [40]
Rnd 14: (sc in next 9 st, inc in next st) repeat 4 times [44]
Rnd 15 – 20: sc in all 44 st [44]
Embroider the nose and the mouth

with black yarn. Insert the safety eyes between rounds 14 and 15, with an interspace of 18 stitches. Embroider cheeks with pastel pink yarn.
Rnd 21: (sc in next 9 st, dec) repeat 4 times [40]
Rnd 22: sc in all 40 st [40]
Rnd 23: (sc in next 8 st, dec) repeat 4 times [36]
Rnd 24: (sc in next 4 st, dec) repeat 6 times [30]
Rnd 25: (sc in next 3 st, dec) repeat 6 times [24]
Stuff the head firmly with fiberfill.
Rnd 26: (sc in next 2 st, dec) repeat 6 times [18]
Rnd 27: (sc in next st, dec) repeat 6 times [12]
Rnd 28: dec 6 times [6]
Fasten off, leaving a long tail. Using a tapestry needle, weave the yarn tail through the front loop of each remaining stitch and pull tight to close. Weave in the yarn end.

BODY

(in off-white)

Start with the neck. Ch 18. Make sure your chain isn't twisted. Insert the hook in the first chain stitch and join the foundation chain with a slst. Continue working in a spiral.

Rnd 1 – 2: sc in all 18 st [18]

Rnd 3: sc in next 8 st, inc in next 2 st, sc in next 8 st [20]

Rnd 4: sc in all 20 st [20]

Rnd 5: ch 15. Place the stitch marker in the next stitch you'll make, this marks the beginning of the next round. Crochet back on the chain, inc in second ch from the hook, sc in next 13 ch, sc in the stitch where the foundation chain starts, continue on the neck and sc in next 20 st, continue on the other side of the chain and sc in next 13 st, inc in next st [51]

Rnd 6: sc in next st, inc in next st, sc in next 22 st, inc in next st, sc in next st, inc in next st, sc in next 23 st, inc in next st [55]

Rnd 7: inc in next st, sc in next st, inc in next st, sc in next 50 st, inc in next st, sc in next st [58]

Rnd 8: sc in next st, inc in next st, sc in next 2 st, inc in next st, sc in next 23 st, inc in next st, sc in next 2 st, inc in next st, sc in next 24 st, inc in next st, sc in next st [63]

Rnd 9: sc in next st, inc in next st, sc in next 3 st, inc in next st, sc in next 54 st, inc in next st, sc in next 2 st [66]

Rnd 10 – 18: sc in all 66 st [66]

LEGS

We have to divide the work to crochet the four legs.

FIRST BACK LEG

First, find the middle back stitch of the lamb body. If you are not there yet, continue crocheting until that point. Then, sc in next 2 st. Place a stitch marker in the next stitch.

Sc in next 10 st, ch 8. Join the last ch and the stitch with the stitch marker by working a slst.

The leg will be formed with 10 sc of the body and the ch-8 foundation chain. Continue working the first back leg:

Rnd 1: sc in next 18 st (10 on the body and 8 on the chain) [18]

Rnd 2 – 3: sc in all 18 st [18]

Rnd 4: sc in next 16 st, dec [17]

Rnd 5: sc in all 17 st [17]

Rnd 6: sc in next 15 st, dec [16]

Rnd 7: sc in all 16 st [16]

Rnd 8: sc in next 14 st, dec [15]

Rnd 9 – 10: sc in all 15 st [15]

Rnd 11: (sc in next st, dec) repeat 5 times [10]

Rnd 12: dec 5 times [5]

Fasten off, leaving a long tail. Using a tapestry needle, weave the yarn tail through the front loop of each remaining stitch and pull tight to close. Weave in the yarn end.

FIRST FRONT LEG

Count 9 stitches along from the first back leg (this will become the belly) and attach off-white yarn to the 10th stitch.

Sc in next 10 st, ch 8 and join the last ch and the first sc stitch with a slst.

Rnd 1 – 12: repeat rounds 1-12 of the first back leg.

SECOND FRONT LEG

Count 4 st to the left of the first front leg (this is the space between the legs) and attach off-white yarn to the 5th stitch.

Sc in next 10 st, ch 8 and join the last ch and the first sc stitch with a slst.

Rnd 1 – 12: repeat rounds 1-12 of the first back leg.

SECOND BACK LEG

Count 9 st to the left of the second front leg (this is the other side of the belly) and attach off-white yarn to the 10th stitch.

Sc in next 10 st, ch 8 and join the last ch and the first sc stitch with a slst.

Rnd 1 – 12: repeat rounds 1-12 of the first back leg.

BELLY

Between the legs you have 9 stitch spaces along the sides and 4 stitch spaces at the front and back.
Make the belly by crocheting flaps on these stitches. Start with the 9 stitch spaces along the side. Attach off-white yarn to the first stitch next to the first leg you made. Crochet in rows.

Row 1 – 12: sc in next 9 st, ch 1, turn [9]

Fasten off, leaving a long tail for sewing.

FLAP BETWEEN THE LEGS

For the back flap, attach off-white yarn to the first stitch next to the last leg you made. Crochet in rows.
Row 1 – 4: sc in next 4 st, ch 1, turn [4]
Fasten off, leaving a long tail for sewing. Work the flap between the front legs in the same way.

ASSEMBLY OF THE BODY

Using a tapestry needle, sew the front flap to both front legs and the back flap to both back legs. Stuff each leg firmly with fiberfill. Using a tapestry needle, sew the wide belly flap to the other side of the lamb. Then sew the belly flap to both legs and the flaps between them, stuffing the body as you go. Sew the head to the body.

EARS

(make 2, start in off-white)
Rnd 1: start 6 sc in a magic ring [6]
Rnd 2: sc in all 6 st [6]
Continue working with alternating yarns (off-white and pastel pink). The color you work with is indicated before each part.
Rnd 3: *(off-white)* (sc in next st, inc in next st) repeat 2 times, *(pastel pink)* sc in next st, inc in next st [9]
Rnd 4: *(off-white)* (sc in next 2 st, inc in next st) repeat 2 times, *(pastel pink)* sc in next 2 st, inc in next st [12]
Rnd 5: *(off-white)* (sc in next 3 st, inc in next st) repeat 2 times, *(pastel pink)* sc in next 3 st, inc in next st [15]
Rnd 6: *(off-white)* (sc in next 4 st, inc in next st) repeat 2 times, *(pastel pink)* sc in next 4 st, inc in next st [18]
Rnd 7 – 14: *(off-white)* sc in next 12 st, *(pastel pink)* sc in next 6 st [18]
Rnd 15: *(off-white)* (sc in next 4 st, dec) repeat 2 times, *(pastel pink)* sc in next 4 st, dec [15]
Rnd 16: *(off-white)* (sc in next 3 st, dec) repeat 3 times [12]
Fasten off, leaving a long tail for sewing. Do not stuff. Flatten and pinch the ears. Sew the ears to the top of the head.

TAIL

(in off-white)
Rnd 1: start 6 sc in a magic ring [6]
Rnd 2 – 5: sc in all 6 st [6]
Fasten off, leaving a long tail for sewing. Do not stuff.

CAPE

(with 2 strands of fingering weight yarn in green, using a size D-3 /3.25 mm crochet hook)
Ch 33. Crochet in rows.
Row 1: start in second ch from the hook, sc in all 32 st, ch 2, turn [32]
Row 2: (hdc in next 7 st, hdc inc in next st) repeat 4 times, ch 2, turn [36]
Row 3: (hdc in next 8 st, hdc inc in next st) repeat 4 times, ch 2, turn [40]
Row 4: (hdc in next 9 st, hdc inc in next st) repeat 4 times, ch 2, turn [44]
Row 5: (hdc in next 10 st, hdc inc in next st) repeat 4 times, ch 2, turn [48]
Row 6: (hdc in next 11 st, hdc inc in next st) repeat 4 times, ch 2, turn [52]
Row 7: (hdc in next 12 st, hdc inc in next st) repeat 4 times, ch 2, turn [56]
Row 8: (hdc in next 13 st, hdc inc in next st) repeat 4 times, ch 2, turn [60]
Row 9: (hdc in next 14 st, hdc inc in next st) repeat 4 times, ch 2, turn [64]
Row 10: hdc in next 4 st, ch 10, skip 10 st, hdc in next st, inc in next st, (hdc in next 15 st, hdc inc in next st) repeat 2 times, hdc in next 2 st, ch 10, skip 10 st, hdc in next 3 st, hdc inc in next st, ch 2, turn [68]
Row 11: hdc in all 68 st, ch 2, turn [68]
Row 12: (hdc in next 16 st, hdc inc in next st) repeat 4 times, ch 2, turn [72]
Row 13: hdc in all 72 st [72]
Without turning, ch 1, sc in the row-ends up the first side (about 13 sc), ch 21 to make the cape straps, start in second ch from the hook, slst in next 20 ch, sc in the stitch where the foundation chain starts, continue on the neckline and sc in next 32 st, ch 21 to make the other cape strap, start in second ch from the hook, slst in next 20 ch, sc in the stitch where the foundation chain starts, sc down the row-ends on the other side (about 13 sc), slst in next 72 st across row 13 of the cape. Fasten off and weave in the yarn ends.

RUFFLE COLLAR
(with 2 strands of fingering weight yarn in pastel pink, using a size D-3 /3.25 mm crochet hook)

Join the pastel pink yarn by inserting the hook in the neckline, with the right side facing you. Crochet in rows.

Row 1: sc in next 32 st, ch 2, turn [32]

Continue working in a stripe pattern in tapestry crochet, making 3 st in pastel pink and 1 st in off-white yarn.

Row 2: hdc inc in all 32 st, ch 2, turn [64]

Continue working in a stripe pattern, making 1 st in off-white and 5 st in pastel pink yarn.

Row 3: (hdc in next st, hdc inc in next st) repeat 32 times [96]

Fasten off and weave in the yarn ends.

Elena Deer

Elena works as an IT freelancer for Nira Tigress: she programs all the systems that help her friend make her ingenious fabrics. When Elena is not working in the lab, she gets her creative kick from programming video games, her true passion. Elena loves video games. They allow her to be whoever she wants to be without always having to be the sweet and lovable deer everyone expects her to be. Work at the lab can get busy and stressful, so to get back on her feet, Elena has taken a couple of months off her day job to work on an exciting new game together with Newton Owl and her soul mate Audrey Gazelle.

GALLERY: Scan or visit *www.amigurumi.com/3120* to share pictures and find inspiration.

Size:
12.5 inches / 32 cm tall when made with the indicated yarn (standing, ears included)

Materials:
– Worsted weight yarn in
 · mink brown
 · off-white
 · black
 · coral
 · pastel pink (leftover)
 · bright red
 · salmon pink
 · yellow (leftover)
– Size C-2 / 2.75 mm crochet hook
– Black safety eyes (8 mm)
– Fiberfill

Skills needed: magic ring *(page 32)*, working around a foundation chain *(page 34)*, working in rows, changing color at the beginning of a round *(page 35)*, working tapestry crochet from a diagram *(page 36)*, dividing the body in 4 parts *(page 158)*, embroidery *(page 38)*, joining parts *(page 39)*

HEAD

(start in black)
Rnd 1: start 6 sc in a magic ring [6]
Rnd 2: inc in all 6 st [12]
Rnd 3: (sc in next st, inc in next st) repeat 6 times [18]
Rnd 4 – 5: sc in all 18 st [18]
Change to off-white yarn.
Rnd 6: sc in all 18 st [18]
Rnd 7: (sc in next 2 st, inc in next st) repeat 6 times [24]
Rnd 8 – 9: sc in all 24 st [24]
Change to mink brown yarn.
Rnd 10: sc in next 9 st, inc in next 6 st, sc in next 9 st [30]
Rnd 11: sc in all 30 st [30]
Rnd 12: sc in next 10 st, (inc in next st, sc in next st) repeat 6 times, sc in next 8 st [36]
Rnd 13 – 14: sc in all 36 st [36]
Rnd 15: sc in next 11 st, (inc in next st, sc in next 2 st) repeat 6 times, sc in next 7 st [42]
Rnd 16 – 17: sc in all 42 st [42]
Rnd 18: (sc in next 6 st, inc in next st) repeat 6 times [48]
Rnd 19: sc in next 18 st, inc in next st, sc in next 10 st, inc in next st, sc in next 18 st [50]
Rnd 20 – 25: sc in all 50 st [50]
Insert the safety eyes between rounds 18 and 19, with an interspace of 18 stitches.
Embroider pastel pink cheeks below the eyes and off-white lines on the head.
Rnd 26: sc in next 18 st, dec, sc in next 10 st, dec, sc in next 18 st [48]
Rnd 27: (sc in next 6 st, dec) repeat 6 times [42]
Rnd 28: sc in all 42 st [42]
Rnd 29: (sc in next 5 st, dec) repeat 6 times [36]
Rnd 30: (sc in next 4 st, dec) repeat 6 times [30]
Rnd 31: (sc in next 3 st, dec) repeat 6 times [24]

Stuff the head firmly with fiberfill.

Rnd 32: (sc in next 2 st, dec) repeat 6 times [18]

Rnd 33: (sc in next st, dec) repeat 6 times [12]

Rnd 34: dec 6 times [6]

Fasten off, leaving a long tail. Using a tapestry needle, weave the yarn tail through the front loop of each remaining stitch and pull tight to close. Weave in the yarn end.

BODY

(start in mink brown)

Start with the neck. Ch 20. Make sure your chain isn't twisted. Insert the hook in the first chain stitch and join the foundation chain with a slst. Continue working in a spiral.

Rnd 1 – 2: sc in all 20 st [20]

Rnd 3: sc in next 9 st, inc in next 2 st, sc in next 9 st [22]

Rnd 4: sc in all 22 st [22]

Rnd 5: sc in next 10 st, inc in next st, sc in next st, inc in next st, sc in next 9 st [24]

Rnd 6: sc in next st, ch 14. Place the stitch marker in the next stitch you'll make, this marks the beginning of the next round. Crochet back on the chain, inc in second ch from the hook, sc in next 12 ch, sc in the stitch where the foundation chain starts, continue on the neck and sc in next 24 st, continue on the other side of the chain and sc in next 12 st, inc in next st [53]

Rnd 7: inc in next 2 st, sc in next 23 st, inc in next st, sc in next 2 st, inc in next st, sc in next 22 st, inc in next 2 st [59]

Rnd 8: (sc in next st, inc in next st) repeat 2 times, sc in next 52 st, inc in next st, sc in next st, inc in next st [63]

Rnd 9: sc in next st, inc in next st, sc in next 2 st, inc in next st, sc in next 25 st, inc in next st, sc in next 3 st, inc in next st, sc in next 24 st, inc in next st, sc in next 2 st, inc in next st [69]

Rnd 10: inc in next st, sc in next 4 st, inc in next st, sc in next 58 st, inc in next st, sc in next 4 st [72]

Rnd 11 – 20: sc in all 72 st [72]

LEGS

We have to divide the work to crochet the four legs.

FIRST BACK LEG

First, find the middle back stitch of the deer body. If you are not there yet, continue crocheting until that point. Then, sc in next 2 st. Place a stitch marker in the next stitch. Sc in next 10 st, ch 8. Join the last ch and the stitch with the stitch marker by working a slst.

The leg will be formed with 10 sc of the body and the ch-8 foundation chain. Continue working the first back leg:

Rnd 1: sc in next 18 st (10 on the body and 8 on the chain) [18]

Rnd 2 – 4: sc in all 18 st [18]

Rnd 5: sc in next 16 st, dec [17]

Rnd 6: sc in all 17 st [17]

Rnd 7: sc in next 15 st, dec [16]

Rnd 8: sc in all 16 st [16]

Rnd 9: sc in next 14 st, dec [15]

Rnd 10: sc in all 15 st [15]

Change to off-white yarn.

Rnd 11: sc in next 13 st, dec [14]

Rnd 12: sc in all 14 st [14]

Rnd 13: sc in next 12 st, dec [13]

Rnd 14: sc in all 13 st [13]

Change to black yarn.

Rnd 15: sc in next 11 st, dec [12]

Rnd 16 – 17: sc in all 12 st [12]

Rnd 18: dec 6 times [6]

Fasten off, leaving a long tail. Using a tapestry needle, weave the yarn tail through the front loop of each remaining stitch and pull tight to close. Weave in the yarn end.

FIRST FRONT LEG

Count 12 stitches along from the first back leg (this will become the belly) and attach mink brown yarn to the 13th stitch.

Sc in next 10 st, ch 8 and join the last ch and the first sc stitch with a slst.

Rnd 1 – 18: repeat rounds 1-18 of the first back leg.

SECOND FRONT LEG

Count 4 st to the left of the first front leg (this is the space between the legs) and attach mink brown yarn to the 5th stitch.

Sc in next 10 st, ch 8 and join the last ch and the first sc stitch with a slst.

Rnd 1 – 18: repeat rounds 1-18 of the first back leg.

SECOND BACK LEG

Count 12 st to the left of the second front leg (this is the other side of the belly) and attach mink brown yarn to the 13th stitch.

Sc in next 10 st, ch 8 and join the last ch and the first sc stitch with a slst.

Rnd 1 – 18: repeat rounds 1-18 of the first back leg.

BELLY

Between the legs you have 12 stitch spaces along the sides and 4 stitch spaces at the front and back. Make the belly by crocheting flaps on these stitches. Start with the 12 stitch spaces along the side. Attach mink brown yarn to the first stitch next to the first leg you made. Crochet in rows.

Row 1 – 12: sc in next 12 st, ch 1, turn [12]

Fasten off, leaving a long tail for sewing.

FLAP BETWEEN THE LEGS

For the back flap, attach mink brown yarn to the first stitch next to the last leg you made. Crochet in rows.

Row 1 – 4: sc in next 4 st, ch 1, turn [4]

Fasten off, leaving a long tail for sewing. Work the flap between the front legs in the same way.

ASSEMBLY OF THE BODY

Using a tapestry needle, sew the front flap to both front legs and the back flap to both back legs. Stuff each leg firmly with fiberfill. Using a tapestry needle, sew the wide belly flap to the other side of the deer. Then sew the belly flap to both legs and the flaps between them, stuffing the body as you go. Sew the head to the body.

TAIL

(in mink brown)

Rnd 1: start 5 sc in a magic ring [5]

Rnd 2: sc in all 5 st [5]

Rnd 3: inc in all 5 st [10]

Rnd 4: sc in all 10 st [10]

Rnd 5: (sc in next st, inc in next st) repeat 5 times [15]

Rnd 6: sc in all 15 st [15]

Rnd 7: (sc in next 3 st, dec) repeat 3 times [12]

Fasten off, leaving a long tail for sewing. Flatten the tail before sewing. The tail does not need to be stuffed.

BONNET HAT

(in coral yarn)

Ch 40. Crochet in rows.

Row 1: start in third ch from the hook, hdc in next 38 st, ch 2, turn [38]

Row 2: hdc in next 38 st, ch 2, turn [38]

Row 3: hdc in next 9 st, ch 6, skip 6 st, hdc in next 8 st, ch 6, skip 6 st, hdc in next 9 st, ch 2, turn [38]

Row 4 – 6: hdc in next 38 st, ch 2, turn [38]

Row 7: hdc in next 18 st, hdc inc in next 2 st, hdc in next 18 st, ch 2, turn [40]

Row 8: hdc in next 19 st, hdc inc in next 2 st, hdc in next 19 st, ch 1, turn [42]

Row 9: sc in next 10 st, hdc in next 22 st, sc in next 10 st [42]

Without turning, ch 1, sc in the row-ends up the first side (about 12 sc), ch 1. Continue across the bottom of row 1, sc in next 38 st, ch 1. Continue down the row-ends on the other side (about 12 sc). Fold the hat in half and slst loosely in each st across the top of row 9, working through both layers of fabric, taking one loop from each row (BLO from the nearest and FLO from the farthest). Fasten off and weave in the yarn ends. Make a 2 inches / 5 cm pompon with salmon pink yarn.

EARS

(make 2, in mink brown)

Rnd 1: start 6 sc in a magic ring [6]

Rnd 2: inc in all 6 st [12]

Rnd 3: sc in all 12 st [12]

Rnd 4: (sc in next st, inc in next st) repeat 6 times [18]

Rnd 5 – 6: sc in all 18 st [18]

Rnd 7: (sc in next 2 st, inc in next st) repeat 6 times [24]

Rnd 8 – 11: sc in all 24 st [24]

Rnd 12: (sc in next 6 st, dec) repeat 3 times [21]

Rnd 13 – 14: sc in all 21 st [21]

Rnd 15: (sc in next 5 st, dec) repeat 3 times [18]

Rnd 16 – 17: sc in all 18 st [18]

Fasten off, leaving a long tail for sewing. Embroider off-white stripes on the inside of the ears. Do not stuff. Flatten and pinch the ears before sewing them on the head.

BLANKET

Note: *For the blanket I use the tapestry crochet technique, following the diagram. If you are not confident using this technique, you can choose to crochet the entire blanket in one color or in a simple stripe pattern.*

(start in off-white)
Ch 31. Crochet in rows. Continue in a gingham pattern working tapestry crochet, using off-white, pastel pink and bright red yarn (see the diagram).
Row 1: start in second ch from the hook, sc in next 30 st, ch 1, turn [30]
Row 2 – 10: sc in all 30 st, ch 1, turn [30]
Without turning, slst an edge all around the blanket with off-white yarn. Fasten off and weave in the yarn end.

Blanket strap (in yellow)
Ch 24. Crochet in rows.
Row 1: start in second ch from the hook, sc in next 23 st, ch 1, turn [23]
Row 2 – 4: sc in all 23 st, ch 1, turn [23]
Fasten off, leaving a long tail for sewing. Sew the strap ends to the blanket.

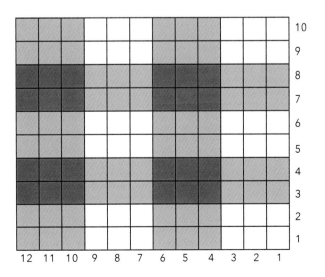

174

ACKNOWLEDGEMENTS

Thanks to my family. Thanks to my children who are my most fervent admirers and acute critics. To Goros, my husband and best friend who pushes me to keep going whenever I want to give up (by being a bit of a buzzing voice in my head). He's also the one who taught me to set up the camera to take relatively decent pictures.
Thanks to Lucas, my partner in the new, crazy adventure of making yarns. Thank you for being almost as crazy as I am, for taking care of all the things I do not like doing (like being a grown-up capable of doing business) and for your trust in me.
Thanks to Joke and Dora, my editors, for continuing to support my ideas, for listening to all my whims and for making my thoughts a little more readable.
Thanks to all pattern testers who helped prepare the patterns for this book, when i first saw one of the finished toys, I was super excited and emotional. It was the moment when the book became 'real' for me. Thank you for your priceless help!
And, as I can't repeat enough, thanks to all of you who are still here, reading my words, encouraging me, sending me love, caring about my problems and sharing pictures of their beloved ones hugging their wonderful creations.
A thousand times, thank you.